Funny Peculiar

BARBARA SLEIGH

Illustrated by Jennie Garratt

DAVID & CHARLES
NEWTON ABBOT LONDON VANCOUVER

ISBN 0 7153 6816 8

Photoset and printed
in Great Britain by
REDWOOD BURN LIMITED
Trowbridge & Esher
for David & Charles (Holdings) Limited
South Devon House Newton Abbot Devon

Published in Canada by Douglas David &
Charles Limited 3645 McKechnie Drive
West Vancouver BC

Contents

Foreword

Have you ever heard anyone say: 'Do you mean funny peculiar, or funny ha-ha?'

My dictionary describes 'funny' as: 'Something comical, affording fun . . .' Then it goes on: 'curious, queer, perplexing, hard to account for.'

It is the second part that this book is about. In it you will find a mixture of strange fiction, and equally strange facts: of odd happenings in space, of ghosts and hauntings, both imaginary and actually experienced: of unsolved mysteries and curious customs: of old beliefs in magic, medicine and folk-lore. Here and there 'ha-ha' funny may mix with the other kind. However, whether the tales told puzzle, surprise, or make your hair stand on end, I hope you will agree they are 'funny peculiar'.

Barbara Sleigh

An old prayer from Cornwall that might well be found useful by the readers of this book.

> From Witches and Wizards
> And long-tailed buzzards
> And creeping things that run along hedge bottoms
> Good Lord Deliver us!

Monsters

Monsters

When is a monster not a monster?

I suppose when it is caught and studied by scientists, given a solemn, latin name, even shut up in a zoo.

Monsters come in all sizes.

When the Spaniards first landed in South America, the Indians were terrified by what they thought to be an invasion of monsters who galloped like the wind, each one with a man-shaped body from the waist upwards sprouting from its back. Only when they saw the creatures at close quarters did they realise they were not all in one piece, but four-legged animals with men riding on their backs. They had never seen a horse before, let alone a man riding one. They were monsters no longer.

The Abominable Snow-Man of our own time has been seen by no one. But what creature leaves the enormous footmarks which are sometimes found in the snows of the Himalayas? Some people say that it is nothing but a large bear – but no one knows for certain. The Sherpas still believe it is the monstrous Yeti which roams above the snow-line. After all, the Sherpas are the men on the spot. They should know when a bear is not a bear.

You are unlikely to find any of the monsters described here in any zoo. Someone at some time has believed in nearly all of them, though one or two, I suspect, were invented as a leg-pull. Scotland has its own monster even today, and there are all the signs of a Gremlin having taken up residence in my kitchen. I should never be surprised to see one . . . but there, one of the characteristics of Gremlins is that they are invisible.

Grendal

The story of Beowulf, and how he slew the terrible monster Grendal, is one of the oldest poems in any modern language. Rosemary Sutcliff has retold the story with her usual skill. This extract tells how for twelve years the monster Grendal visited the great hall of Heorot, and slew the warriors sleeping there, until the coming of Beowulf.

Grendal, the Night Stalker, Grendal, the Man-Wolf, the Death Shadow, who has his lair among the sea inlets and the coastal marshes. He heard the laughter and the harp-song from the King's high hall, and it troubled him in his dark dreams, and he roused and came up out of the waste lands and snuffed about the porch. The door stood unfastened in the usual way – though it would have been little hindrance to him had it been barred to keep out a war-host . . .

Grendal prowled in, hating all men and all joy, and hungry for human life. So swift was his attack that no man heard an outcry; but when the dawn came, thirty of Hrothgar's best and noblest thanes were missing, and only the blood splashed on walls and floors, and the monster's footprints oozing red, remained to tell their fate . . .

Many times happened this dreadful slaughter, until the coming of the warrior Beowulf.

And then in the darkest hour one spring night, Grendal came to Heorot as he had come so many times before, up from his lair and over the high moors, through the mists that seemed to travel with him under the pale moon; Grendal, the Night-stalker, the Death Shadow. He came to the fore-porch and snuffed about it, and smelled the man-smell, and found that the door that had been unlatched for him so long was barred and bolted. Snarling with rage that any man should dare attempt to keep him out, he set the flat of his talon-tipped hands against the timbers and burst them in.

Dark as it was, the hall seemed to fill with a monstrous shadow at his coming; a shadow in which Beowulf, half springing up, then holding himself in frozen stillness, could make out no shape nor clear outline save two eyes filled with a wavering greenish flame.

The ghastly corpse-light of his own eyes showed Grendal the shapes of men as it seemed to him sleeping, and he did not notice among them one who leaned upon his elbow. Laughing in his throat, he reached out and grabbed young Hondscio who lay nearest to him, and almost before his victim had time to cry out, tore him limb from limb and drank the warm blood. Then, while the young warrior's dying shriek still hung upon the air, he reached for another. But this time his hand was met and grasped, seized in a grasp such as he had never felt before; a grasp that had in it the strength of thirty men.

Beowulf leapt from the sleeping-bench and grappled him in the darkness; and terror broke over Grendal in full force, the terror of the wild animal trapped; so that he thought no more of his hunting but only of breaking the terrible hold upon his arm and flying back into the night and the wilderness, and he howled and bellowed as he struggled for his freedom. Beowulf set his teeth and summoned all his strength and tightened his grip until the sinews cracked; and locked together they reeled and staggered up and down the great hall. Trestles and sleeping-benches went over with crash on crash as they strained this way and that, trampling even through the last, red embers of the dying fire; and the very walls seemed to groan and shudder as though the stout timbers would burst apart. And all the while Grendal snarled and shrieked and Beowulf fought in silence save for his gasping breaths.

Outside the Danes listened in horror to the turmoil that seemed as though it must burst Heorot asunder; and within, the Geats had sprung from their sleeping-benches, sword in hand, forgetful of their powerlessness against the Troll-kind, but in the dark, lit only by stray gleams of bale-fire from the monster's eyes, they dare not strike for fear of slaying their leader, and when one or other of them did contrive to get in a blow, the sword glanced off Grendal's charmed hide as though he was sheathed in dragon's scales.

At last, when the hall was wrecked to the walls, the Night-Stalker gathered himself for one last, despairing effort to break free. Beowulf's hold was as ever; yet none the less the two figures burst apart – and Grendal with a frightful shriek staggered to the doorway and through it, and fled wailing into the night, leaving his arm and shoulder torn from the roots in the hero's still-unbroken grasp.

Beowulf sank down sobbing for breath on a shattered bench and

his fellows came crowding round him with their torches rekindled at the scattered embers of the fire; and together they looked at the thing he held across his knees. 'Not even the Troll-kind could live half a day with a wound such as that upon them,' one of them said; and Waegmund agreed. 'He is surely dead as though he lay here among the benches.'

'Hondscio is avenged, at all events,' said Beowulf. 'Let us hang up this thing for a trophy, and a proof that we do not boast idly as the wind blows over.'

So in triumph they nailed up the huge, scaly arm on one of the roof beams above the High Seat of Hrothgar.

From *Beowulf, Dragon Slayer* by Rosemary Sutcliff

Jabberwocky

'Twas brillig, and the slithy toves
    Did gyre and gimble in the wabe:
All mimsy were the borogroves,
    And the mome raths outgrabe.

'Beware the Jabberwock, my son!
    The jaws that bite, the claws that catch!
Beware the Jubjub bird, and shun
    The frumious Bandersnatch!'

He took his vorpal sword in hand:
    Long time the manxome foe he sought –
So rested he by the Tumtum tree,
    And stood awhile in thought.

And, while in uffish thought he stood,
    The Jabberwock with eyes of flame,
Came whiffling through the tulgey wood,
    And burbled as it came!

One, two! One, two! And through and through
    The vorpal blade went snicker-snack!
He left it dead, and with its head
    He went galumphing back.

'And hast thou slain the Jabberwock?
    Come to my arms my beamish boy!
O frabjous day! Callooh! Callay!'
    He chortled in his joy.

'Twas brillig, and the slithy toves
    Did gyre and gimble in the wabe:
All mimsy were the borogroves,
    And the mome raths outgrabe.

Lewis Carroll

The Scub

Unfortunately Noah did not leave an inventory of the animals on board the Ark. Kenneth Walker and Geoffrey Boumphrey, in their book *The Log of the Ark*, describe a remarkably unpleasant creature called 'The Scub', which they imagine might have slipped on board uninvited. They tell of the effect it had on the other animals in the course of the voyage, especially on the Seventy-Sevens. These were two shy little creatures about the size of a rabbit, with eyes as big as a calf's who, because they could not remember what they were, were called by their cabin number.

In the days of which this speaks, sometime before the flood, the Scub had been much as other beasts – a happy, light-hearted fellow who loved to bask in the light of the sun, or romp free of care 'neath the full moon. To him one day as he lay dozing had come a rabbit, frisking about with the joy of life; who, seeing the Scub asleep across his path, made to jump over his outstretched neck.

But some evil chance at that instant caused the Scub to open his eyes, and in the confusion of awakening, seeing he knew not what, hurtling through the air at him, he snapped at it. There was a thin squeal, and he felt in his jaws the little rabbit – dead, with its back broken, and on his lips, for the first time, the taste of blood! A moment he paused, and in that moment all the evil that was in him swept over him like a flood. Glancing guiltily round, he fell upon the little body and devoured it with horrid snarls.

From that day the life of the Scub began to change. He grew to hate the light; and, leaving the sunny plains, went to live in a gloomy cavern among the hills, where he could find food of the kind nearest to what he craved – a blood-red, fleshy toadstool, that grew in the damp, rotting places of the rocks. And soon the rumour of his deed sprang to life – none knew whence – and spread among the beasts, until his name was spoken with loathing and then not at all.

Behold him now, and mark well how the body, grown loathsome, bore witness to the life he had lived. His colour – once a brave, burnished green – had blanched to a pale, sickly yellow, like the dank, oozing fungus among which he had chosen to live. His body – once lithe and strong to gambol in the sun – had sunk and grown flabby with the years of foul living. His head – once held proudly erect, but now on sagging neck scarce off the ground – waved unceasingly from side to side as he peered around. Yet was all this as nothing to the evil of his face. Great, pale eyes, too weak to bear the light of day, shuttered with heavy lids that never opened wide – nightmare eyes that looked none straight in the face, yet ever seemed to watch and leer and gloat. The mouth – wide, loose-cornered, with thin slobbery lips that writhed a little and twitched, while from the upper hung two, limp, fleshy feelers, forever quivering and shaking.

Such, then, was the Scub, whom Japhet saw now, crouching in the darkest corner of a cabin in the darkest part of the Ark.

'Hello,' he said. 'I haven't seen you before, have I?'

'I think not,' replied the Scub in an oily voice.

'How is that?' asked Japhet.

'I fancy it was rather late when I came on board, and I did not

like to disturb you,' answered the Scub, with a horrible attempt at pleasantness.

'What is your name, then?'

'I am called the Scub.'

'I don't seem to have heard of you at all,' said Japhet, looking puzzled, 'and I am almost certain you are not in my natural history book.'

'Very likely not,' explained the Scub. 'You see, I live in the hills, and I go out very little. I really find the crowded life here most distressing.'

'Well, I suppose it's all right,' said Japhet, 'but I think you might have told someone. What have you done about meals? I haven't seen you up there.'

'I ventured to take possession of a vacant seat,' returned the Scub, with an oily smile. 'But I find the bright light very trying to my eyes; and I took the liberty, therefore, of selecting one as much in the shadow as possible.'

'Oh, well, all right,' said Japhet, and went away to find Noah. 'Father,' he said, 'I've just found another animal on board that I don't know anything about. He's perfectly horrible-looking, but seems quite polite – a bit too polite, I think. I got shivers down my back every time he spoke. Have you ever heard of a Scub, father?'

'Scub? now let me see,' pondered Noah. 'I seem to recollect my father telling me something about a beast of that name. Now whatever was it? Something rather bad, if I remember rightly. Still, let us not harbour evil thoughts against anyone, my son. It is all a very long time ago. Have you given him a cabin?'

And so the Scub came to be accepted in the Ark, and of all on board only the Wise Marabou Stork took any notice. 'Mark my words,' he said to the Old Black Bear, 'he is an evil beast, and no good will come of it. Would that I could remember what my father said, when he warned me against him.'

'Umph!' said the Old Bear.

For some time all went well on the Ark, but as the days lengthened into weeks, first the Old Marabou Stork, and then everyone on board, began to notice the change which was making its presence felt more and more every day. The beasts still played about on deck or bathed, or dozed away the hours in the hot sun; but there was a difference. No longer were they the great, big, happy family that they had been before. Something of the old comradeship had gone, and in its place was something new and evil. Very gradually the animals began to divide into different sets. They would sit in groups apart, and stop talking when other beasts passed by. This could be seen most plainly with the Tigers and the Leopards, who glared openly at any Deer or Sheep daring to speak to them or even come near.

The Fox, too, who had been a witty, friendly sort of fellow, began to keep himself to himself, and to be full of mysterious journeyings too and fro. There was a curious story told by an Owl. In the middle of one night this Owl had wakened, and seen the Fox in the birds' quarters. He was sitting on his haunches, as quiet as a mouse, gazing fixedly at two sleeping Fowls. The Owl had hooted, and at the sound the Fox had disappeared noiselessly into the shadows.

At this time it would have been difficult to connect the Scub in any way with the changes which were taking place. He did not grumble nearly so much as the Camel; and yet there was something in his smug and smarmy way of talking that upset people, so that everywhere he went he left an unpleasant feeling behind him. Always he moved from one group of animals to another, dropping a few words, which never seemed to mean quite what they said, and then slinking quietly away, as though he had work to be done elsewhere.

Especially he was to be seen with the great Cats – the Tigers, Lions, Leopards and Panthers – flattering them, and making them prouder and more stand-offish than ever; while who could say what evil suggestions were hatched in the dark corners where he would lie, talking earnestly to his cronies the Wolves, the Foxes, and the Weasels.

Of all on board only the Stork, who was on the look-out for it, realised the mischief that the Scub was making. And yet, despite his never-failing politeness, there rose among the gentler beasts, even the larger ones, such as the Kangaroo, the Deer, and the Hippopotamus himself, a vague distrust.

'There's something about that chap I don't like,' said the Hippopotamus one day.

'Nor do I,' said the Elephant. 'He makes me feel all creepy,' and she glanced nervously behind her.

'What's he want to go buttering up them great, silly cats for?' added the Hippopotamus. 'They're quite stuck-up enough already, without making them worse.'

'It isn't only them. I can't think what's come over everybody,' said the Kangaroo plaintively. 'I must have said "Good-morning" to a score of people today, and hardly a soul would give me a civil answer.'

'It's quite true,' said the Red Deer. 'It makes me feel quite queer to go near those Tigers – the way they look·at you. Everyone

seems to be as cross as cross.'

'I believe it's all that Scub's doing,' declared the Kangaroo. 'I found the two Seventy-Sevens this morning sobbing in a corner as though their hearts would break. They said they'd heard the Scub talking in his sleep – their cabin is next to his, you know – but they wouldn't tell me what he said.'

'Funny how he seems to have scared all the little 'uns,' said the Hippopotamus.

And then one night there was commotion in the Ark.

'What is all this noise about?' broke in a voice from the end of the passage, and Shem made his way along, followed by Ham and Japhet.

'The Elephant thinks someone has fallen overboard,' said the Camel.

'Well, why don't you go and look instead of arguing?' cried Shem, turning and hurrying back.

'What a good idea,' said the Yak. 'That will prove it,' and he joined the other animals who were rushing on deck to see what it was that had made the splash that the Elephant had heard while dropping off to sleep.

Up on deck it was almost as light as day, for a great, round moon was hanging overhead and turning all the little waves to silver. When the Yak got out, it was to find Ham, Shem and Japhet, and as many animals as there was room for leaning eagerly over the rail and gazing down into the water outside the Elephant's cabin.

'There's no sign of anyone now,' said Shem. 'Are you sure you weren't dreaming?'

'I'm absolutely positive,' said the Elephant indignantly. 'I was – why – what's that?' she broke off excitedly, and pointed with her trunk. About fifty yards away on the shining water was what looked to the Elephant's weak eyes like a round, dark patch; but there were those with far better sight than hers. Everyone looked. 'It's a tub or something,' said Shem.

'And there's somebody in it,' said the Tiger, who like all cats could see splendidly at night. 'I think it – ' but he stopped suddenly and listened; for, stealing across the water to the silent listeners on the Ark, came the sound of two little voices singing – rather chokily, and very out of tune, if tune there was:

> 'We'll slip from the Ark,
> While the night is dark;
> And we'll sail away
> To the break of day;
>> For we're safe in our tub
>> From the fear of the Scub.
>
> 'We're not very bold;
> And the water's cold;
> And we haven't a sail,
> Yet we'll row with our tail;
>> For we're safe in our tub
>> From the fear of the Scub,'

There was not a move nor a sound from the group on the Ark, till the last word of the song had faded into silence.

'It's the poor, little Seventy-Sevenses,' said Japhet at last.

On deck no one had moved. All were straining their ears to catch the words which came so faintly over the water that only the Elephant and one or two others could make them out:

'Our food for a week'll
Be scrapings of treacle;
And water, we think,
Will be plenty to drink;
    For we're safe in our tub
    From the fear of the Scub.

'So though we don't know
Where we're going, we'll go;
And hope that the light
Will show land in sight.
    For safe is our tub
    From fear of the Scub.'

And that was the last that anybody heard. But still they kept their places, and watched the little, dark patch on the shining water, until it became a speck, and then a tiny, tiny dot e'er it disappeared for ever.

Then very quietly and sadly, the animals turned and went back to their cabins. As they went Shem spoke: 'Is the Scub there?' he said – but there was no reply.

Adapted from *The Log of the Ark* by Kenneth Walker and Geoffrey Boumphrey

The Salamander

It has been recorded that some people have actually seen creatures that we think of as mythical.

Benvenuto Cellini was a famous goldsmith who lived in the sixteenth century. He kept a diary, from which this account of a salamander is taken.

When I was about five, my father was sitting alone singing and playing his viol. Some washing had just been done there and a good, log fire was still burning. It was very cold and he had drawn near the fire. Then, as he was looking at the flames, his eye fell on a little animal, like a lizard, that was running around merrily in the very hottest part of the fire. Suddenly, realising what it was, he called my sister and myself and showed it to us. And then he gave me such a violent box on the ears that I screamed and burst into tears. At this he calmed me as kindly as he could and said:

'My dear little boy, I didn't hit you because you had done wrong, I did it so you will never forget that the lizard you saw in the fire is a salamander, and as far as we know for certain no one has ever seen one before.' Then he kissed me, and gave me a little money.

From the *Autobiography of Benvenuto Cellini*, 1500–71

Mythical Monsters

The Unicorn

This is not to be confused with the Bicorne, for it has a single horn growing from the centre of its forehead. It is otherwise shaped in the manner of a white horse. The horn has magical properties. It is very potent against poison, and will purify water no matter how foul. It is said that Queen Elizabeth I had a drinking cup made from the horn of a unicorn.

The Bunyip

According to Australian legend, this creature lived in streams and pools and boggy places, and lived on the flesh of men. The female was even more to be feared than the male. Should any man threaten her child, she would at once cause a flood to rise. When the creeping water touched the feet of her enemy, he would be turned into a swan.

Devil's Dandy Dogs

The Cornish name for a pack of fire-breathing hounds, black as night, and with glowing eyes, which goes hunting with the Devil on stormy nights.

The Bicorne

A two-horned creature which was first recorded in the sixteenth century. It lived only on the flesh of hen-pecked husbands, but was always sleek and well fed.

The Catolepas

This animal is first mentioned by Pliny, in the first century, and was found in Ethiopia. It was a small, slothful animal, who nevertheless dealt death to anyone unfortunate enough to see its eyes. Luckily its head was so heavy that it seldom raised its eyes from the ground.

Gremlins

These were first noted by the Royal Naval Air Service in World War I. They were said to look like a cross between a rabbit and a bull-dog. They were in the habit of causing all manner of unforeseen, mechanical mishaps, particularly upsetting the balance of aeroplanes, so that the airman was sometimes forced to bale out. Their favourite food is petrol, and to this day, wherever there is machinery of any kind, from computers and space-ships to vacuum-cleaners and spin-dryers, they are very much in evidence, although the modern kind is invisible.

Goofus

This creature was discovered by lumber-jacks in North America. It was solely interested in scenes it had visited before, and so only flew backwards. Its nests are built upside down.

The Mewlips

The shadows where the Mewlips dwell
    Are dark and wet as ink,
And slow and softly rings their bell,
    As in the slime you sink.

You sink into the slime, who dare
    To knock upon their door,
While down the grinning gargoyles stare
    And noisome waters pour.

Beside the rotting river-strand
    The drooping willows weep,
And gloomily the gorcrows stand
    Croaking in their sleep.

Over the Merlock Mountains a long and weary way,
    In a mouldy valley where the trees are grey,
By a dark pool's borders without wind or tide,
    Moonless and sunless, the Mewlips hide.

The cellars where the Mewlips sit
    Are deep and dank and cold
With single, sickly candle lit;
    And there they count their gold.

Their walls are wet, their ceilings drip;
    Their feet upon the floor
Go softly with a squish-flap-flip,
    As they sidle to the door.

They peep out slyly; through a crack
    Their feeling fingers creep,
And when they've finished, in a sack
    Your bones they take to keep.

Beyond the Merlock Mountains, a long and lonely road,
   Through the spider-shadows and the marsh of Tode,
And through the wood of hanging trees and the gallows-weed,
   You go to find the Mewlips – and the Mewlips feed.

From *The Adventures of Tom Bombadil* by J. R. R. Tolkien

Pterodactyls

These were prehistoric creatures, whose existence has been proved by the discovery of a number of skeletons. Conan Doyle describes what they must have been like in his book *The Lost World*, in which Professor Challenger and his fellow explorers discover a strange plateau which has been completely cut off from the passing of time, and is still inhabited by prehistoric animals.

Creeping to his side, we looked over the rocks. The place into which we gazed was a pit, and may, in the early days, have been one of the smaller volcanic blow-holes of the plateau. It was bowl-shaped, and at the bottom, some hundreds of yards from where we lay, were pools of green-scummed, stagnant water, fringed with bulrushes. It was a weird place in itself, but its occupants made it seem like a scene from the Seven Circles of Dante's Hell. The place was a rookery of pterodactyls. There were hundreds of them congregated within view. All the bottom area round the water-edge was alive with their young ones, and with hideous mothers brooding upon their leathery, yellowish eggs. From this crawling, flapping mass of obscene, reptilian life came the shocking clamour which filled the air and the mephitic, horrible, musty odour which turned us sick. But above, perched each upon its own stone, tall, grey, and withered, more like dead and dried specimens than actual, living creatures, sat the horrible males, absolutely motionless save for the rolling of their red eyes or an occasional snap of their rat-trap beaks as a dragon-fly went past them. Their huge, membranous wings were closed by folding their fore-arms, so that they sat like gigantic, old women, wrapped in hideous, web-coloured shawls, and with their ferocious heads protruding above them. Large and small, not less than a thousand of these filthy creatures lay in the hollow before us.

Our professors would gladly have stayed there all day, so entranced were they by this opportunity of studying the life of a prehistoric age. They pointed out the fish and dead birds lying about among the rocks as proving the nature of the food of these creatures, and I heard them congratulating each other on having cleared up the point why the bones of this flying dragon are found in such great numbers in certain, well-defined areas, as in the Cambridge Greensand, since it was now seen that, like penguins, they lived in gregarious fashion.

Finally, however, Challenger, bent upon proving some point which Summerlee had contested, thrust his head over the rock and nearly brought destruction upon us all. In an instant the nearest male gave a shrill, whistling cry, and flapped its twenty-foot span of leathery wings as it soared up into the air. The females and young ones huddled together beside the water, while the whole circle of sentinels rose one after the other and sailed off into the sky. It was a wonderful sight to see at least a hundred creatures of such enormous size and hideous appearance all swooping like swallows with swift, shearing wing-strokes above us: but soon we realised that it was not one on which we could afford to linger. At first the great brutes flew round in a huge ring, as if to make sure what the exact extent of the danger might be. Then, the flight grew lower and the circle narrower, until they were whizzing round and round us, the dry, rustling flap of their huge, slate-coloured wings filling the air with a volume of sound that made me think of Hendon aerodrome upon a race day.

'Make for the wood and keep together,' cried Lord John, clubbing his rifle. 'The brutes mean mischief.'

The moment we attempted to retreat, the circle closed in upon us, until the tips of the wings of those nearest to us nearly touched our faces. We beat at them with the stocks of our guns, but there was nothing solid or vulnerable to strike. Then suddenly out of the whizzing, slate-coloured circle a long neck shot out, and a fierce beak made a thrust at us. Another and another followed.

Summerlee gave a cry and put his hand to his face, from which the blood was streaming. I felt a prod at the back of my neck, and turned dizzy with the shock. Challenger fell, and as I stopped to pick him up, I was again struck from behind and dropped on the top of him. At the same instant, I heard the crash of Lord John's elephant-gun, and, looking up, saw one of the creatures with a broken wing struggling upon the ground, spitting and gurgling at us with a wide-opened beak and blood-shot, goggled eyes, like some devil in a medieval picture. Its comrades had flown higher at the sudden sound, and were circling above our heads.

'Now,' cried Lord John, 'Now for our lives!'

We staggered through the brushwood, and even as we reached the trees, the harpies were on us again. Summerlee was knocked down, but we tore him up and rushed among the trunks. Once there we were safe, for those huge wings had no space for their sweep beneath the branches. As we limped homewards, sadly mauled and discomfited, we saw them for a long time flying at a great height against the deep blue sky above our heads, soaring round and round, no bigger than wood-pigeons, with their eyes no doubt following our progress. At last, however, as we reached the thicker woods they gave up the chase, and we saw them no more.

From *The Lost World* by Sir Arthur Conan Doyle

Travellers' Tales

Travellers' Tales

So long as there is anything left to discover, there will always be an audience for tales told by brave men who have travelled further than the rest of us, whether on the other side of the world, or in outer space, and who have seen strange things.

Only two of these extracts are told with the teller's tongue pushed firmly in his cheek. You must judge whether they are stranger tales than some of the true ones.

In 1322, Sir John Maundeville set out to discover the best route for pilgrims to follow who were travelling to Jerusalem, the Holy City. His wanderings took him more than thirty years. This is an extract from the account of his discoveries written on his return. Perhaps you may wonder whether he really believed such strange things. After all, there are people today who believe in little, green men from Mars, which is no more surprising. You must remember too, that in 1322, three-quarters of the world was as remote and uncharted as Mars is to us today.

The Voyages and Travels of Sir John Maundeville

. . .Going by sea towards the south, is an island called Dondun. . . The king of this island is a great and powerful lord, and has under him fifty-four great isles, which give tribute to him; and everyone of these islands has a king crowned, all obedient to that king. In one of these isles are people of great stature, like giants, hideous to look upon; and they have but one eye which is in the middle of the forehead, and they eat nothing but raw flesh and fish. And in another isle towards the south dwell people of foul stature and cursed nature who have no heads, but their eyes are in their shoulders.

In another isle are people who have the face all flat, without nose and without mouth. In another isle are people that have the lip

above the mouth so great, that when they sleep in the sun they cover all the face with that lip. And in another isle there are dwarfs, which have no mouth, but instead of their mouth they have a little round hole; and when they shall eat or drink, they take it through a pipe, or a pen, or such a thing, and suck it in. And in another isle are people that have ears so long that they hang down to their knees. And in another isle are people that have horses' feet. And in another isle are people that go upon their hands and feet like beasts, and are all skinned and feathered, and would leap as lightly into trees as squirrels or apes . . . And in another isle are people that go always upon their knees, and at every step they go it seems that they would fall; and they have eight toes on every foot. Many other divers people of divers natures there are in other isles about, of the which it were too long to tell.

From *The Voyages & Travels of Sir John Maundeville*

Squids

Thor Heyerdahl, with a parrot and five companions, set out on the
Kon-Tiki, a raft made of balsa wood, to sail across the Pacific. He
set out to prove that the original inhabitants of the Polynesian
Islands could have come in the same way from Peru. As you would
expect, their adventures with sea creatures were many and various.

The marine creature against which the experts had begged us to be
most on our guard was the octopus, for it could get on board the
raft. The National Geographical Society in Washington had
shown us reports and dramatic, magnesium photographs from an
area in the Humboldt Current where monstrous octopuses had
their favourite resort and came up on the surface at night. They
were so voracious that if one of them fastened on to a piece of meat
and remained on the hook, another came and began to eat its cap-
tured kinsman. They had arms which could make an end of a big
shark and set ugly marks on great whales, and a devilish beak like
an eagle's hidden among their tentacles. We were reminded that
they lay floating in the darkness with phosphorescent eyes, and
that their arms were long enough to feel about in every small
corner of the raft, dragging us out of our sleeping-bags at night,
and we provided ourselves with sabre-like, machete knives, one
for each of us, in case we should wake to the embrace of groping
tentacles. There was nothing which seemed more disagreeable to
us when we started, especially as the marine experts in Peru got on
to the same subject and showed us on the chart where the worst
area was, right in the Humboldt Current itself.

For a long time we saw no sign of a squid, either on board or in
the sea. But then one morning we had the first warning that they
must be in those waters. When the sun rose, we found the progeny
of an octopus on board, in the form of a little baby the size of a cat.
It had come up on deck unaided in the course of the night and lay
dead with its arms twined round the bamboo outside the cabin
door. A thick, black, inky liquid was smeared over the bamboo
deck and lay in a pool round the squid. We wrote a page or two in

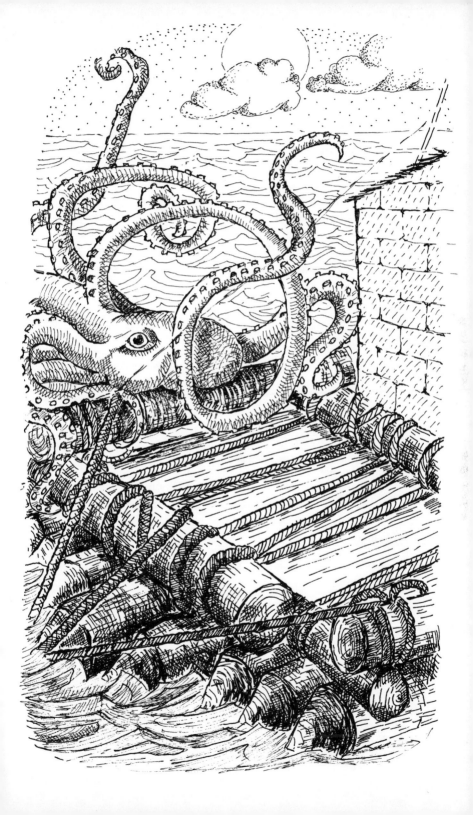

the log-book with cuttle-fish ink, which was like Indian ink, and then flung the baby overboard for the pleasure of the dolphins.

We saw in this minor incident the harbinger of larger night visitors. If the baby could clamber on board, its hungry progenitor could no doubt do the same. Our forefathers must have felt the same as we when they sat in their Viking ships and thought of the Old Man of the Sea. But the next incident completely bewildered us. One morning we found a single, smaller, young squid on the top of the roof of palm leaves. This puzzled us very much. It could not have climbed up there, as the only ink marks were smeared in a ring round it in the middle of the roof. Nor had it been dropped by a sea bird, for it was completely intact, with no beak-marks. We came to the conclusion that it had been flung up on the roof by a sea which had come on board, but none of those on night watch could remember any such sea that night. And as the nights passed, we regularly found more young squids on board, the smallest of them the size of one's middle finger.

It was soon usual to find a small squid or two among the flying fish about the deck in the morning, even if the sea had been calm in the night. And they were young ones of the real, devilish kind, with eight, long arms covered with sucking discs and two still longer with thorn-like hooks at the end. But large squids never gave a sign of coming on board. We saw the shine of phosphorescent eyes drifting on the surface on dark nights, and on one single occasion we saw the sea boil and bubble while something like a big wheel came up and rotated in the air, while some of our dolphins tried to escape by hurling themselves desperately through space. But why the big ones never came on board, when the small ones were constant night visitors, was a riddle to which we found no answer.

Young squids continued to come aboard. One sunny morning we all saw a glittering shoal of something which shot up out of the water and flew through the air like large rain-drops, while the sea boiled with pursuing dolphins. At first we took it for a shoal of flying fish, for we had already had three different kinds of these on board. But when they came near, and some of them sailed over the raft at a height of four or five feet, one ran straight into Bengt's chest and fell slap on the deck. It was a small squid. Our astonishment was great. When we put it into a sailcloth bucket it kept on taking off and shooting up to the surface, but it did not develop speed enough in the small bucket to get more than half out of the water. It is a known fact that the squid ordinarily swims on the principle of the rocket-propelled aircraft. It pumps sea-water with great force through a closed tube along the side of the body, and can thus shoot backwards in jerks at a high speed; and with all its tentacles hanging behind it in a cluster over its head, it becomes stream-lined like a fish. It has on its sides two, round, fleshy folds of skin which are ordinarily used for steering and quiet swimming in the water. But it was thus shown that defenceless young squids, which are a favourite food of many large fish, can escape their pursuers by taking to the air in the same way as flying fish. They had made the principle of the rocket aircraft a reality long before human genius hit upon the idea. They pump sea-water through themselves till they get up a terrific speed, and then they steer up at an angle from the surface by unfolding the pieces of skin like wings. Like the flying fish, they make a glider-flight over the waves for as far as their speed can carry them. After that, when we had to begin to pay attention, we often saw them sailing along for fifty to sixty yards, singly and in twos and threes. The fact that cuttlefish can 'glide' has been a novelty to all the zoologists we have met.

As the guest of natives in the Pacific, I have often eaten squid; it tastes like a mixture of lobster and India rubber. But on board the *Kon-Tiki*, squids came last on the menu. If we got them on the deck gratis we just exchanged them for something else. We made the exchange by throwing out a hook with the squid on it, and pulling it in again with a big fish kicking at the end of it. Even tunny and bonito liked young squids, and they were food which came at the head of our menu.

From *The Kon-Tiki Expedition* by Thor Heyerdahl

Who Discovered America?

If I asked you 'Who discovered America?' I expect you would say, 'Why, Christopher Columbus, of course.'

But there are some people who would not agree. There is a theory that America was discovered by Norsemen many years before Columbus; another, that it was Amerigo Vespucci. But there is a stranger legend about a Welsh prince called Madoc.

The story goes that Madoc set sail from his homeland in 1170, either as a penance or to escape the war-like quarrelling of his eighteen brothers, over which of them should rule over the North of Wales when their father, Owain Gwynedd, died. His ship was the *Gwennan Gorn*, and her sides were made of good, Welsh oak held together with stags' horns instead of nails, so that they could not rust. She sailed away towards the West in search of new lands.

For two years, no more was heard of her, and doubtless the eighteen brothers thought she had sunk with all hands in a storm in an unknown sea, or fallen prey to some great sea monster – or even fallen off the edge of the world: for this was in the days when everyone thought the earth was as flat as a plate. But after two years the *Gwennan Gorn* came back. You might think by now Madoc would be sick of sea-faring, but not a bit of it. He stayed only long enough to raise a larger fleet and both men and women volunteers, before returning to the far-off land he had discovered. Once more he sailed into the West, and this time no more was heard of him or his brave fleet.

Now we come to the curious part of the story.

In the seventeenth and eighteenth centuries, when pioneers were exploring North America, a tribe of Red Indians was discovered whose skins were white, and whose hair was fair, and who spoke a language very like Welsh. Could these 'Indians' be the descendants of Prince Madoc and his band who had landed in Alabama in 1170? A number of people were convinced that this must be so. In 1953, a

tablet was put up on the shores of Mobile Bay with the inscription:
'IN MEMORY OF PRINCE MADOC, A WELSH EXPLORER, WHO
LANDED ON THE SHORES OF MOBILE BAY IN 1170, AND LEFT
BEHIND WITH THE INDIANS THE WELSH LANGUAGE.'

Barbara Sleigh

Adventure with a Leopard

Charles Kingsley, the author of *The Water Babies,* had a niece
called Mary. For thirty years she lived the quiet, enclosed life you
would expect of a Victorian lady, but on the death of both her
parents in 1893, to the astonishment of her friends, she set out,
alone, to explore West Africa, still wearing the bonnet and ankle-
length skirts in fashion at the time. Among Africans she became a
legend.

Here is one of her surprising adventures.

Once, in the bush, as she and her party came in to a village, they
found a leopard caught in a game trap by some kind of snare;
struggling, snarling and roaring as one can well imagine. The
African method was to leave it till it wore itself to death; but when
night came, and Mary Kingsley shut herself up in her allotted hut,
the cries of the magnificent creature became more than she could
bear. Going out into the dark she found herself in terror because
she had not stayed to put on boots, and the chances of walking on a
snake were formidable. Africans never moved about by night,
probably for this reason.

When she reached the trap, guided by the leopard's eyes, blaz-
ing like lamps in the dark, she set to the business of pulling out the
stakes (of the trap) keeping away as best she could from her captive, though in one of his frantic dashes he ripped her skirt from top
to bottom. But she accomplished her object of pulling away all but
the last stake, which she reckoned that the leopard would be able
to pull for himself. She was right: he did. But then to her dismay,

instead of bolting into the jungle as she expected, he came and began to walk round her, sniffing at her. She was frightened with a vengeance. Fear, however, had its usual effect on her; instead of bolting she said firmly, 'Go home you fool!' And the leopard went.

A moment after, she heard a violent rustling in the tree behind her; something dropped with a thud, and then she was aware of it crawling round her feet. It was one of the Fan hunters, who had seen her go out and followed her, and when he saw her go up to the trap, thought the best place was up a tree. When he heard her speak to the leopard and saw it obey her, he concluded that she was some sort of god and came down to make obeisance.

From *The Life of Mary Kingsley* by Stephen Gwynn

A Surprising Adventure of Baron Munchausen

I once set off from Rome on a journey to Russia, in the midst of
winter. I went on horseback, as the most convenient manner of
travelling. It had been snowing hard one day when night and
darkness overtook me. No village was to be seen. The country was
covered with snow, and I was unacquainted with the road.

   Tired, I alighted, and fastened my horse to something, like a
pointed stump of a tree, which appeared above the snow: for the
sake of safety I placed my pistols under my arm and laid down on

the snow where I slept so soundly that I did not open my eyes till full day light. It is not easy to conceive my astonishment to find myself in the midst of a village, lying in a churchyard; nor was my horse to be seen, but I heard him, soon after, neigh somewhere above me. On looking upwards I beheld him hanging by his bridle to the weather cock of the steeple.

Matters were now very plain to me: the village had been covered with snow overnight; a sudden change of weather had taken place; I had sunk down to the churchyard whilst asleep, gently, and in the same proportion as the snow had melted away; and what, in the dark, I had taken to be the stump of a little tree appearing above the snow, to which I had tied my horse, proved to have been the cross or weathercock of the steeple.

Without long consideration, I took one of my pistols, shot the bridle in two, brought down the horse and proceeded on my journey.

From *Baron Munchausen, Narrative of His Marvellous Travels* by Rudolph Raspe

Hints for Spies

Sir Robert Baden-Powell, the founder of the Boy Scout Movement, travelled to Dalmatia – the name now given to the coast of Yugoslavia – and invented an ingenious method of openly making drawings of fortifications without awakening anyone's suspicions.

Butterfly Hunting in Dalmatia
Once I went 'butterfly hunting' in Dalmatia. I went armed with the most effective weapons for the purpose, which have served me well in many a similar campaign. I took a sketch-book, in which were numerous pictures – some finished, some partly done – of butterflies of every degree and rank, from a 'Red Admiral' to a 'Painted Lady'.

Carrying this book and a colour-box, and a butterfly net in my hand, I was above all suspicion to anyone who met me on the lonely mountain-side, even in the neighbourhood of the forts.

I was hunting butterflies, and it was always a good introduction with which to go to anyone who was watching me with suspicion. Quite frankly, with my sketch-book in my hand, I would ask innocently whether he had seen such-and-such a butterfly in the neighbourhood, as I was anxious to catch one.

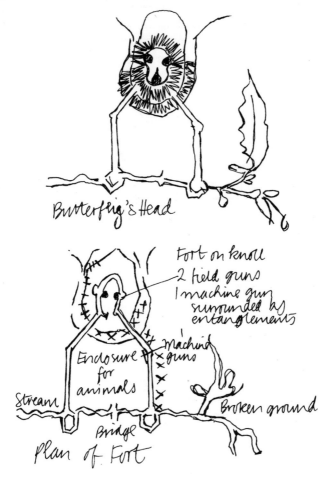

Concealing a Fort in a Moth's Head

This sketch was made, giving all particulars that I wanted. I then decided to bury it in such a way that it could not be recognised as a fortress plan if I were caught by the fortress authorities. One idea occurred to me was to make it into the doorway of a cathedral, or a church, but I finally decided on the sketch of a moth's head. Underneath I wrote the following words:

'Head of Dula moth as seen through a magnifying glass. Caught 19.5.12. Magnified about six times the size of life.'
    (Meaning scale of 6 inches to the mile)
This sketch of a butterfly contains the outline of a fortress, and

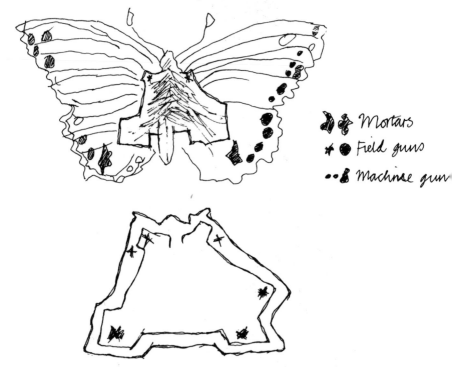

marks both the position and power of the guns, according to the keys below.

The marks on the wings show the shape of the fortress shown in the second drawing, and the size of the guns. The position of each gun is at the place inside the outline of the fort on the butterfly, where the line marked·with the spot ends. The head of the butterfly points towards the north.

Ninety-nine out of a hundred did not know one butterfly from another – any more than I do – so one was on fairly safe ground in that way, and they thoroughly sympathised with the mad Englishman who was hunting these insects.

They did not look sufficiently closely into the sketches to notice that the delicately-drawn veins of the wings were exact representations, in plan, of their own fort, and that the spots on the wings denoted the number and position of guns and their calibres.

From *Advice to Spies* by Sir Robert Baden-Powell

Typee

On New Year's Day, 1841, Herman Melville signed on the whaling ship, *Acushnet*, but after eighteen months he could stand no more. He based his book, *Typee,* on his adventures during his escape with a shipmate, Tobias Green. They fell in with a tribe of natives, on the Marquesas Islands, the Typee. Melville suspected that they were cannibals, but at first saw nothing to confirm this.

I proposed to Kory-Kory, the young man appointed.as my servant, that, according to our usual custom in the morning, we should take a stroll to the Ti, the meeting hut: he positively refused; and when I renewed the request, he evinced his determination to prevent my going there; and, to divert my mind from the subject, he offered to accompany me to the stream. We accordingly went, and bathed. On our coming back to the house, I was surprised to find that all its inmates had returned, and were lounging upon the mats as usual, although the drums still sounded from the groves.

The rest of the day I spent with Kory-Kory and Fayaway, wandering about a part of the valley situated in an opposite direction from the Ti, and whenever I so much as looked towards that building, although it was hidden from view by intervening trees, and at the distance of more than a mile, my attendant would exclaim, 'Taboo, taboo!' [forbidden]

At the various houses where we stopped, I found many of the inhabitants reclining at their ease, or pursuing some light occupation, as if nothing unusual were going forward; but amongst them all I did not perceive a single chief or warrior. When I asked several of the people why they were not at the 'Hoolah Hoolah' (the feast), they uniformly answered the question in a manner which implied that it was not intended for them, but for Mehevi, Narmonee, Mow-Mow, Kolor, Womonoo, Kalow, running over, in their desire to make me comprehend their meaning, the names of all the principal chiefs.

Everything, in short, strengthened my suspicions with regard to the nature of the festival they were now celebrating; and which amounted almost to a certainty. While in Nukuheva I had frequently been informed that the whole tribe were never present at these cannibal banquets, but their chiefs and priests only; and everything I now observed agreed with the account.

The sound of the drums continued without intermission the whole day, and falling continually upon my ear, caused me a sensation of horror which I am unable to describe. On the following day, hearing none of those noisy indications of revelry, I concluded that the inhuman feast was terminated, and feeling a kind of morbid curiosity to discover whether the Ti might furnish any evidence of what had taken place there, I proposed to Kory-Kory to walk there. To this proposition he replied by pointing with his finger to the newly-risen sun, and then up to the zenith, intimating that our visit must be deferred until noon. Shortly after that hour we accordingly proceeded to the taboo groves, and as soon as we entered their precincts, I looked fearfully round in quest of some memorial of the scene which had so lately been acted there; but everything appeared as usual. On reaching the Ti, we found Mehevi and a few chiefs reclining on mats, who gave me as friendly a reception as ever. No allusions of any kind were made by them to the recent events; and I refrained, for obvious reasons, from referring to them myself.

After staying a short time, I took my leave. In passing along the piazza, previously to descending from the pi-pi, I observed a curiously carved vessel of wood, of considerable size, with a cover placed over it, of the same material, and which resembled in shape a small canoe. It was surrounded by a low railing of bamboos, the top of which was scarcely a foot from the ground. As the vessel had been placed in its present position since my last visit, I at once con-·cluded that it must have some connexion with the recent festival; and, prompted by a curiosity I could not repress, in passing it I raised one end of the cover; at the same moment the chiefs, perceiving my design, loudly ejaculated, 'Taboo! taboo!' But the slight glimpse sufficed; my eyes fell upon the disordered members of a human skeleton, the bones still fresh with moisture, and with particles of flesh clinging to them here and there!

Kory-Kory, who had been a little in advance of me, attracted by the exclamations of the chiefs, turned round in time to witness the expression of horror on my countenance. He now hurried towards me, pointing at the same time to the canoe, and exclaiming, rapidly, 'Puarkee! puarkee!' (Pig) I pretended to yield to the deception and repeated the words after him several times, as though acquiescing in what he said. The other savages, either deceived by my conduct, or unwilling to manifest their displeasure at what could not now be remedied, took no further notice of the occurrence, and I immediately left the Ti.

All that night I lay awake, revolving in my mind the fearful situation in which I was placed. The last horrid revelation had now been made, and the full sense of my condition rushed upon my mind with a force I had never before experienced.

From *Typee* by Herman Melville

The Big Rock Candy Mountains

One evening as the sun went down
And the jungle fire was burnin'
Down the track came a hobo hikin',
And he says: 'Boys, I'm not turnin'
I'm headed for a land that's far away
Beside the crystal fountains,
So come with me, and we'll go see
The Big Rock Candy Mountains.

'In the Big Rock Candy Mountains,
There's a land that's fair and bright,
Where the handouts grow on bushes,
And you sleep out every night.
Where the boxcars are all empty,
And the sun shines every day
On the birds and the bees, and the cigarette trees,
And the lemonade springs where the bluebird sings,
In the Big Rock Candy Mountains.

'In the Big Rock Candy Mountains
The cops have wooden legs,
The bulldogs all have rubber teeth,
And the hens lay soft-boiled eggs.
The farmer's trees are full of fruit,
And the barns are full of hay.
Oh, I'm bound to go where there ain't no snow
Where the rain don't pour, and the wind don't blow,
In the Big Rock Candy Mountains.

'In the Big Rock Candy Mountains
You never change your socks,
And the little streams of alcohol
Come trickling down the rocks.
Where the brakemen have to tip their hats
And the railroad bulls are blind.
There's a lake of stew and of whiskey too,
You can paddle all around 'em in a big canoe,
In the Big Rock Candy Mountains.

'In the Big Rock Candy Mountains
All the jails are made of tin,
And you can bust right out again
As soon as you are in.
There ain't no short-handled shovels,
No axes, saws or picks,
I'm going to stay where you sleep all day,
Where they hung the Turk who invented work,
In the Big Rock Candy Mountains.'

Anon

Unsolved Mysteries

The Man in the Iron Mask

In 1703, in the fortress prison of the Bastille, there died a prisoner who had been shut away within its grim walls for five years. He was given no name, and what he looked like nobody knows, for he wore a mask at all times, some say made of iron and some of velvet on an iron frame. He had previously been imprisoned, first at Pignerol, and then on the Isle of Sainte Marguerite, making in all twenty-four, long years of imprisonment, during which time no one had ever seen his face. On his death, his room in the Bastille was deliberately gutted, so that no trace of his identity could possibly remain. The furniture was destroyed and the walls scraped bare of any markings. Even the floor boards were pulled up and burned, with his few, personal possessions. The prison records, that might have shed some light on his mystery, were destroyed when the Bastille was taken during the French Revolution. Nothing remained but the legend of his tragic imprisonment. As time went on, he became known all over Europe as the Man in the Iron Mask.

All that is known for a fact is that the governor of all three of the prisons in which the unhappy captive was held, was the same man. His name was Saint-Mars. When Saint-Mars was promoted from Pignerol, first to be governor of the prison on the Isle of Sainte Marguerite and later to the Bastille – perhaps as a reward for keeping his mouth shut about his strange, heavily guarded prisoner – the Man in the Iron Mask followed him. It seems that Saint-Mars treated his mysterious captive with some respect, that he provided him with rich clothes, and good food served on silver plates. This much was learned by fellow prisoners, but that was all. They had no speech with him.

There is a story told that when he was a captive on the Isle of Sainte Marguerite, a fisherman, fishing close to the prison walls, drew up in his net something that shone dully among the leaping fish. It was a silver dish. The fisherman recognised the royal coat-of-arms of the Bourbon family on the rim, but he could make nothing of some marks which had been scratched on its surface, which might have been writing: for he could not read. He took it to Saint-Mars. It seems that Saint-Mars gave the fisherman a gold piece, and told him to wipe the whole affair from his memory. Was the writing on the dish an attempt by the unhappy prisoner to tell the world of his plight? Perhaps if the fisherman had been able to read, the future history of the Man in the Iron Mask might have been very different; or if the dish had not been handed to the one person we can only suppose was paid to suppress any knowledge of his existence, the mystery might have been made clear.

But strange mysteries breed strange stories and rumours.

Who was the Man in the Iron Mask? There are many different theories. The most ordinary and perhaps the most likely one is that he was a certain senator of Mantua, who deceived Louis XIV over

a secret treaty for the purchase of the Fortress of Casal. Another, that he was an Armenian church dignitary who had persecuted the Catholics.

Among the stranger stories is one that claims the unhappy prisoner was the English Duke of Monmouth, son of Charles II. Defeated at the battle of Sedgemoor, he was sentenced to be executed on Tower Hill for rebelling against his uncle James II. The story goes that James, having promised his brother to see that no harm came to Monmouth, substituted another prisoner who was executed in his place. Monmouth was then smuggled over to France, where Louis had promised to keep him hidden and out of further mischief. This he did by means of the mask and life-long imprisonment.

Another legend has it that he was the twin brother of Louis XIV. It seems that there was an old prophecy which foretold disaster to the royal family if ever twins should be born to them. According to this story, the second child was spirited away by Louis XIII and brought up secretly by Cardinal Mazarin. Louis XIV, it is said, only discovered his brother's existence by chance after the Cardinal's death, and, fearing a future rival to the throne of France, condemned him to a lifetime of solitary confinement, with his face covered so that the tell-tale likeness to himself should never be seen.

Perhaps the strangest story of all is that the Man in the Iron Mask had a son, who was smuggled away to Corsica, where he was known as Buona Parte, and there founded a family which in its turn was to produce a famous son, Napoleon Bonaparte. The fact that Napoleon tried unsuccessfully to solve the riddle of the Man in the Iron Mask, adds colour, but no proof, to the story.

These are only a few solutions which have been put forward to a mystery that is unlikely ever to be solved. Perhaps the real story of this tragic man was more remarkable than any of them.

Barbara Sleigh

The Mysterious Affair of the Marie Celeste

On 5 December, in the year 1872, the brigantine *Dei Gratia* was sailing from New York with her hold full of cargo, bound for Gibraltar. At three o'clock in the afternoon the look-out reported a sail. Captain Moorhouse, part-owner of the ship, signalled her. On receiving no reply, he ordered the *Dei Gratia* to approach the unresponsive ship, so that he could examine her more closely through his telescope. The more he looked, the more his curiosity was aroused. Her decks and rigging were deserted, and there was no one at her wheel. She was yawing all over the place, with flapping sails; and yet there was no distress signal at her masthead. Sailing as she was hundreds of miles from land, what could possibly be the explanation?

At last the *Dei Gratia* drew near enough for him to read the name on her bows. It was the *Marie Celeste*.

Captain Moorhouse at once called for the first mate.

'Mr Deveau,' he said. 'You will take a boat and boarding party immediately, and find out why there is no sign of life on the brigantine!'

'Ay, ay, sir!' said the mate.

Now it so happened that Captain Moorhouse had a personal reason for his concern. He knew the captain of the *Marie Celeste* quite well, a man called Briggs, and had dined with him shortly before they had both sailed from America a month ago. He knew that Captain Briggs had 1,700 barrels of commercial alcohol aboard – a dangerous cargo – and that his wife and baby daughter travelled with him. It can be imagined with what impatience he awaited the return of the first mate.

'We searched every corner of the ship,' reported Deveau, 'but there was not a soul aboard!'

'And the ship's boat?' asked Captain Moorhouse.

'Gone sir,' said the mate. 'But it's a puzzling thing. There's no

53

sign of a hasty launching. Everything seems in perfect order!'

Then and there, Captain Moorhouse decided to salvage the *Marie Celeste*, to put a party aboard her with the first mate, and sail her to Gibraltar, there to be handed over to the harbour master.

On the long haul to Gib, there was time for further investigation. It seems that the log-book, which records the bare facts of a ship's day-to-day sailing, was in its usual place and had been faithfully kept until ten days before the meeting with the *Dei Gratia*. The last entry gave the ship's position as six miles north-north-east of the easternmost tip of the Azores. If the *Marie Celeste* had been abandoned immediately after this last entry, how could she have sailed as far as the meeting-place with the *Dei Gratia*, with her sails set as they were and flapping forlornly? She must have been manned for some time longer. But in this case, why was there no further entry in the log?

In the captain's cabin, his clothes, and those of his wife, were hanging neatly in their cupboard. There was no sign of disorder, and the captain's watch and some loose change had been left lying by his bunk; just as the crew had gone without taking any of their personal possessions. Even their pipes and tobacco had been left behind, usually a sailor's greatest treasure.

This might mean one of two things. Either that when they had embarked in the ship's boat, they fully intended to return in a short while – this is borne out by the fact that only a small amount of food was missing – and for some reason of rough December weather, they were prevented from getting back. Or else that they left in such a hurry they had no time to pick up even their most precious belongings. But what could have caused such panic?

There were several conflicting clues as to what happened.

First, one of the hatches, the covers of the hold, was misplaced and found lying on its side. Directly below this, one of the barrels of alcohol was damaged. Had the fumes from the broken cask exploded, and blown off the hatch? This might have resulted in the fear that the rest of the cargo was about to explode, which would blow the ship sky-high, and would make a hurried departure necessary. Or had the crew mutinied, and broken the hatch away to get at the alcohol? This solution was borne out by a cutlass lying by the hold, with brown stains on the steel blade, which might have been rust – or blood. If it was mutiny, although they might perhaps have set the captain adrift with his wife and child, surely a mutinous crew would not themselves have left the ship of which they had just gained possession?

Secondly, the sounding-rod, which was used to measure the water-level in the hold, was found lying near the pumps. Were they suddenly afraid that the water-level was rising dangerously fast, so that an immediate escape from the ship was advisable?

Thirdly, part of the ship's rail was cut away. This might possibly have been caused by difficulty in launching the ship's boat, though there has even been the rather wild suggestion that the *Marie Celeste* had been attacked by some hideous sea-monster, and that the axe marks on the rail were made in a desperate fight with it.

Another theory is that Captain Briggs went mad, murdered the crew and threw their bodies overboard and then put to sea. If so he made a very tidy job of it. Except for the cutlass, there was no sign of any other bloodstains, and he had been sane enough to take with him the ship's sextant, which would be needed for navigating, and the ship's papers which were also missing.

Then again, why was there the beginning of a scribbled message on a slate in the handwriting of the mate, apparently to his wife? It began: 'My dear Fanny . . .' and then broke off. What could have interrupted him?

Yet another theory is that the two captains had hatched a plot between them, whereby the *Dei Gratia* should find the *Marie Celeste* abandoned, and that Captain Moorhouse should claim the salvage money which he would then share with Captain Briggs and the crew. But both men were of excellent reputation and unlikely to do anything so dishonest.

Only one thing is certain in this strange affair. Which is that from that day to this, no trace has been found of the ship's boat, with its tragic load of captain, crew, captain's wife and small baby. The mystery of the *Marie Celeste* remains as puzzling today as it was just one hundred years ago.

Barbara Sleigh

The UFO Mystery

It seems that space travel is not a modern invention after all! The people of Taiwan claim that the first people to land on the moon were not the Americans in 1969, but the Emperor Ming of the Tang dynasty in AD 718, together with his astrologer. In the summer of 1973, the island celebrated the 'Moon Cake Festival', in honour of the landing 1,255 years ago, and every prisoner in the jails of Taiwan was presented by the prime minister with a 'Moon Cake'.

Similarly, curious flying objects have been recorded for hundreds of years, in stone carvings, medieval manuscripts and legends. What these apparitions were can only be guessed, but from what is now known, many people believe that they were what we have come to call 'flying saucers'.

In the days when air travel, let alone exploration in outer space, was unheard of, they were described in many ways: 'balls of fire', 'pillars of light', 'flying ships', or 'fiery chariots'; for you must remember that the only means of travelling on land or sea, other than walking, riding on horse-back or swimming, was by ship, chariot, or some kind of coach.

By the eighteenth century, reports of these strange visions became more frequent, and were described in more detail. Even Jacob Grimm, among the folk tales he collected for his *Household Tales*, include a story of a flying ship.

Fifty years ago, just before World War I, 'flying saucers' became news. It was reported in a London newspaper that people in Cardiff and Newport had seen a huge flying object which left a trail of smoke behind it which no one could explain. It had been seen by so many different people that it could not be dismissed as a wild story, and as time went on and more and more reports came in of strange things being seen in the sky, general interest was really aroused.

In 1947, Kenneth Arnold, an American business man, was flying his privately owned plane over the Cascade Mountains, near the north-west Pacific coast of America, when he was surprised to see a chain of nine, saucer-like objects in the sky about twenty miles away. He described them as 'flat like a pie-pan, and so shiny they reflected the sun like a mirror'. He watched them fly out of sight at 1,700mph, an unheard-of speed for those days, but he was an experienced pilot and was convinced that his description was accurate But what had he really seen? Could it have been a deceptive play of sunlight on an unusual cloud formation? Was it, as some thought, a new, Russian, secret weapon? (This was in the days of the Cold War.) Or could it possibly have been an aircraft from another planet?

More and more reports of strange apparitions came in. They had been seen by people of every kind, and it was thought that the time

had come to take them seriously. The United States Air Force set up a project named Blue Book, to investigate the increasingly numerous reports of what the public called 'flying saucers', but which, in official circles, were referred to more cautiously as 'unidentified flying objects', or UFOs. Many of the reports could be dismissed as being caused by weather-balloons, high-flying aeroplanes, vapour trails, meteorites, or even birds, and some of them of course were hoaxes, but many of them could not be explained so easily.

There was, for example, the case of a BOAC Stratocruiser crossing the Atlantic. Both pilot and passengers saw 'a large, round, black object, which kept changing shape like a swimming jellyfish'. From this emerged several, smaller, disc-shaped objects. They kept pace with the Stratocruiser, as though observing it, for a quarter of an hour, then the 'saucers' went back to the large ship and disappeared inside it. It then flew off at an immensely high speed and disappeared.

In August 1954, a Frenchman was coming out of his garage one night after locking up his car, when he saw a huge, luminous object a hundred yards away, hovering over the nearby river. He described it as the shape of a huge cigar standing on end. It was edged with a bright halo of light. This 'thing' also produced smaller, disc-like objects, which in turn hovered with a wobbling motion. This time the discs flew off to the north at a high speed. Meanwhile the parent ship had ceased to glow, and finally faded into the darkness.

It is interesting to find the same descriptions repeatedly turning up: the cigar-shaped object, the wobbling motion and the shining discs.

In 1965, three, American, high-school boys were driving home when they saw what seemed to be a ball of light, about eight feet across, coming rapidly down from the sky. It seemed to hit the ground directly in front of the car before springing back into the sky again. Had the boy who was driving not jammed on his brakes, he said he might have driven straight into whatever it was. Thoroughly frightened, they turned for home again and saw the ball of fire once more, a hundred feet above the ground and head-ing south. When they reported their tale, the authorities were inclined to be sceptical, until an independent account of the same thing seen at the same time was made by other observers.

If these really are aircraft, they must be navigated by some kind of reasoning being. What can these creatures be like? The descriptions given by those who are said to have actually seen them vary. Some describe them as little men, others as very tall. There are even those who say they have spoken to them, eaten with them, and actually ridden in their 'flying saucers'. But these accounts are so contradictory that they prove nothing.

One thing is certain. If *we* can send rockets into outer space, and land men on the moon, it would be unreasonable to deny that the inhabitants of other planets *could* do the same on earth.

Barbara Sleigh

The Loch Ness Monster

This creature is still a mystery. Since the first century, it is reported as having been seen, and the argument as to what it is, or is not, still goes on. Is it some huge survival from prehistoric times? Or is there some more prosaic explanation for these curious appearances?

For hundreds of years there has been a tradition that some strange creature lurks in the waters of Loch Ness. As far back as AD 550 Saint Columba, who brought Christianity to Scotland, is said to have rescued from its clutches a Pict called Lugne. Making the sign of the cross, the Saint commanded the monster, in the name of God, to let go his prey and trouble men no more, and the creature obeyed. But fear of the beast still continued; so much so that children playing on the shores of the loch would choose someone to keep watch, in case it crept up from the water unawares, and stole one of their number away.

The early stories of the monster may have been confused with the belief in the kelpie, a water-spirit who, it was thought, lived in lakes and pools, and delighted in drowning unwary travellers.

Over the last hundred years, so many people, of so many different kinds, have been so sure that they have seen the monster, that it can't be dismissed as mere superstition. With the invention of motor cars, and the building of a road by the side of the loch, widespread interest was aroused, and eye-witness accounts of the creature multiplied. So firm was the belief that the beast really existed, that in 1933 Bertram Mills offered £20,000 to anyone who would deliver the Loch Ness Monster alive to his circus. No one claimed the money.

How do these eye-witness accounts describe the creature? There are several schools of thought, particularly as to its size. Some people have seen it as a single hump, like an up-turned boat, of varying length, from ten feet upwards, while others, equally certain, claim that it is anything up to forty feet long, consisting of a number of humps. These two descriptions do not necessarily disprove one another. The Single-Humpers might have seen only the part of the creature above water, while the rest was submerged. The Many-Humpers claim that the monster is like a gigantic eel, and that the 'humps' are merely the way it propels itself along through the water, rather like a looper caterpillar but with a number of loops. Nearly all observers agree that it has a long, thin neck which rears high out of the lake with a small head; that it moves through the loch at some speed, making a noticeable bow-wave, leaving a wake of churned up water. Some insist that the foam is caused by the fact that it moves by means of paddling itself along with flippers. It is said to sink, when disturbed, with a flurry of foam.

Those who claim to have been near enough to see it clearly say that its colour is dark brown, or elephant grey, with a paler colour underneath, while its surface is described sometimes as smooth and gleaming, and at others as 'knobbly and warty like a toad'.

What is the truth of all this? Nobody yet knows. Of course, there have been hoaxes. One, which caused some excitement at the time, was the discovery of enormous foot-prints on the shore, leading to the exact spot where an observer claimed to have seen the

monster slide into the water. These were later proved to have been made with a dried hippopotamus foot: it was thought of the kind that was sometimes made into an ink-well, as a big game-hunter's trophy, in the days before the biro was invented.

Those who claim that the story of the monster is nonsense, say that what people have really seen is nothing more than a mass of floating rubbish, with the branch of a tree sticking out which has been mistaken for the creature's neck and head. The four rivers which drain into Loch Ness bring down branches, leaves, fallen trees, and all kinds of vegetable matter, which eventually sinks to the bottom of the lake. As it becomes rotten, it produces a marsh gas, which at last forces the matted rubbish to rise to the surface, where the gas explodes, perhaps several times, each explosion producing a 'hump' before the gas escapes, at the same time forcing the mat forwards through the water. Only when the gas has finally dispersed does the sodden mass sink again to the bottom in a swirl of bubbles. This theory does not explain the bow wave, and the speed at which so many say the thing travels.

What sort of animal do those who believe in the monster think it may be? Some say a giant seal, or a walrus which has found its way up through the loch's single outlet; some that it is an enormous eel, or even a crocodile, or that legendary creature the great Kraken itself.

Perhaps the most interesting theory is that it is a plesiosaur, a fish-eating prehistoric reptile which was thought to be extinct. It would not be the first creature to be discovered which it was imagined was extinct, for example, the coelacanth, which was recently discovered in South African waters.

Which of these is your solution?

Barbara Sleigh

Ghosts

The Extra Hand

Do you believe in ghosts?

There are too many stories told by sensible people who declare they have seen them to dismiss the idea entirely as nonsense.

Many tales have been told of haunted ships. Can you guess who, or what, was the 'extra hand'?

I reckon you've heard a dozen and more versions of the 'extra hand' in ships? It was in 1909. I was then a second-year apprentice in the four-masted bark, *Arrow*, flying the flag of the old Anglo-American Oil Company. We pulled out from New York with a capacity freight of case oil for Hong Kong, and we were going the long way, around the Cape of Good Hope, for economy reasons. Time didn't matter so long as our freight reached its destination.

We struck bad weather; midway across the South Atlantic the ship was lifting high and then taking it green and deep as if a pair of giant hands were pressing her down and meant to keep her there. Every once in a while a sea came over us with a roar. It was bad, but it looked like conditions might improve by dawn and we made the best of it. It was raining furiously, and Macdonald, the mate, was in his usual place on the poop, hunched up in oilskins and sou'wester, his eyes peeled like they always were at times like that, watching out for the unexpected, fearing the worst, hoping for the best.

Then he let out a howl: 'Loose those royals and make it snappy!' And as he yelled to us the moon, which was nearing full, came out from behind heavy clouds, a great round moon it was and seemed to be taking a peek at us and enjoying what it saw, which we weren't. Unexpectedly, the wind fell and we settled down to a steady, seven knots or so.

Now, it was my job to loose the mizzen-royal, but I never was as quick on my feet as Macdonald wanted me to be; looking back now I'm prepared to thank the Almighty I wasn't fast enough. So Macdonald yelled an uncomplimentary remark in my direction and ordered a seaman standing near me, a Finn, to get aloft, which he did. A minute later we got the deck hail from our fore and main-royal yards that the canvas was ready for hoisting, which it was, and sheeted home safe.

I was keeping out of the mate's way, which seemed the wisest thing to do, for he never was a sweet-tempered man. I ducked around a deckhouse and watched aloft. Macdonald was watching too, as he always did, expecting to find fault. We could see the Finn on our mizzen-royal quite clearly. He was half-way out on the weather yard but he wasn't doing anything, just still as if he had gone aloft to enjoy the view, and had found it too absorbing to remember he was a seaman. Then a dark tension seemed to come down and surround the ship as if some evil force was about to be let loose. A seaman nearby reckoned it was black magic. It scared me. There was *something* I couldn't put a name to.

Macdonald, mad as they make 'em, strode along the deck and yelled, 'What the blazes is that flamin' Finn doing in the mizzen-royal?'

'Why, 'e ain't doin' nothin' at all, sir,' a seaman replied, grinning like a Cheshire cat; but the mate wiped that grin off his face with a back-hander that sent the seaman spinning on his heels. 'So Mister Flamin' Finn reckons he's on some pleasure boat?' snorts Macdonald. 'Okay *you*!' He waited while the seaman picked himself up dazed. 'Get aloft and give my compliments to that Finn and ask him if he'd be kind enough to step down here and have a word with me. Step lively, man!'

The seaman hadn't gone a couple of feet into the rigging before a regular, doldrum swell, long and oily, came at the ship like silk, under-running her, with pretty near no vestige of real air for a man to draw into his lungs. The bark was swinging drunkenly, groaning like a sick man. In the two years I had been afloat, nothing like this had happened and I had never before felt that strange sensation that surrounded us. The air seemed electric.

Macdonald fretted and fumed and kept watching aloft, and then the seaman he had sent up yelled back for the mate to send up a couple more hands with snatch-block and gantline. The mate, eyes popping out of their sockets, swore and promised trouble if this was some kind of feeble joke; but the two men went aloft with the gear and we watched them go. They edged along toward the Finn and the first man, who appeared to be holding the Finn by his arms; the three of them – and it was obvious from the deck they had to use force – were prying the Finn's fingers from their grip and into a bowline-on-the-bight in that gantline. Then, slowly, very carefully, they lowered him down to the deck.

'What happened up there?' asked the mate.

'He were all glassy-eyed, hanging on to the jackstay like 'is fingers were froze. He's out and that's for sure.'

Macdonald prodded the senseless Finn with the toe of his sea boot, as a man might prod the side of his dog, stirring it to life. But the Finn made no move; only his eyelids flickered. A seaman filled a bucket over the rail, emptied the contents over the Finn. The seawater revived the unconscious man and he sat up weakly and stared around him. Then, as if he'd seen a ghost, he shivered, cowered against the mate's legs and looked up with terrified eyes.

The mate said, 'I sent you aloft to loose the mizzen-royal. Why didn't you?'

'I ban try,' said the Finn. 'I ban try dam' hard . . .'

'You don't have to try, mister, you just do it!'

'I ban try . . .' The Finn's eyes were bad to look into and his lips quivered with real fear. '. . . *but he wouldn't let me!*'

I thought Macdonald was about to have convulsions, for his face darkened and the veins stood out at his temples and neck: 'Who d'ye mean – "he"?'

'Fella with a scar under one eye,' replied the Finn, and passed out again.

Macdonald's face was strained but he quickly recovered his normal, cold composure and turned to the waiting seamen. 'Get him to his bunk. Give him a hot drink. I'll be along.'

We went to the seamen's quarters where the Finn was propped up in his bunk. Macdonald asked him to describe what had happened in the yards and what this 'he' might be the Finn talked about. The Finn told him. A big man, scarred under his left eye, dressed in torn oilskins with a bright sou'wester on his head . . .

Macdonald's face, which had been black and stained with anger a moment ago, suddenly went white, death-white. I noticed it, but

the seamen did not. He gripped my arm and hurried me along to his cabin without speaking. He closed the door once we were inside, unlocked a cabinet on the bulkhead above his bunk, took a long swig from a bottle of rum. 'I needed that like I never needed anything,' he muttered. A thin trickle of sweat began on his temples and slowly ran down his drawn cheeks.

'Listen, son,' he said, moments later, 'I got to tell somebody or it'll drive me crazy. You ever heard tell of the "extra hand" in a ship?' he asked me. I nodded, but said nothing. 'Well, what I'm going to tell you happened during our previous trip in this same ship. The weather was lousy, with seas coming aboard to smash everything movable, until sometimes we carried around a foot of water. Eight days out from New York, it looked like we'd never make it and there wasn't any sense going along. Most of her regular canvas had gone, spares too, but I got the crew rigging temporary sails and bent them on fast as they knew how.

'I was on deck, keeping a weather eye open and alongside me were a couple of seamen to work the capstan. When everything was hoist as best the men could, the two seamen stood by ready to lead the halyard ends to that capstan, and then, without warning, a sea, bigger than any other I've seen, smashed over us and swept everything in its path. The old *Arrow* heeled over until her sticks came almost parallel with the seas. When she righted herself, slowly, so slowly I never thought she'd make it upright again, there he was, lying at my feet, twisted up and his neck broken. His eyes were open, but they had a terrible, anguished look in them. He was dead.'

'Who?' I asked Macdonald.

'French Pete,' he said. Then he lowered his voice to a whisper. 'And you know something, son? French Pete was wearing worn oilskins and a tattered, old, yellow sou'wester. Also, French Pete had a long, curved scar down one cheek he'd got in a maul in a 'Frisco waterfront saloon years back. Dead, I tell you, a full, twelve months ago, and he was up there today, up on our weather yard, and wouldn't let the Finn come one step nearer him!'

From *Sea Phantoms* by Warren Armstrong (W.E. Bennett)

Ghostlore of the Gilbert Islands

The Gilbertese believed that the more recently departed of their relations could and did return. They were jealous. They wanted to see what their descendants were doing. Their skeletons or skulls were preserved in village shrines mainly for them to re-enter if they liked. If skulls at least were not kept, their ghosts would come and scream reproach by night with the voices of crickets, from the palm leaves that over-hung the dwellings. And so, whether a man was pious or impious to his fathers, his house was forever brooded over by unseen watchers.

Not that the older folk thought of their dead only as threatening ghosts. There was love as well as fear in the ancient cult of the

ancestor, and mostly the love predominated. I was looking round the waterfront of a Tarawa village one day, when I came upon an old, old man alone in a canoe-shed nursing a skull in the crook of his elbow. He was blowing tobacco smoke between its jaws. As he puffed he chuckled and talked aloud: 'The smoke is sweet, grandfather,-ke-e-e-!' he was saying. 'We like it? Ke-e-e-e?'

He told me he was loving the skull because his grandfather – who was inside it at that moment – had been very good to him in years gone by. 'Is it not suitable,' he asked, 'for me to be good to him in return?' and answered himself at once, 'Aongkoa!(Of course!)' He went on to say he had chosen tobacco as his offering of love because, as far as he knew, there was no supply of that particular luxury in the ancestral paradise. For his homely affection, at least, the skull was no grim reminder of death, but a cheerful token of man's and love's immortality.

From *A Pattern of Islands* by Sir Arthur Grimble

Toast

I have never seen a ghost that I am aware of, but I think I have *smelt* one.

We used to live in a Victorian, semidetached house in a London suburb. Both houses had pleasant gardens at the back. In the other half of ours lived an old lady, who often woke in the morning as early as half-past four, as old people sometimes do. When she was unable to go to sleep again on summer mornings, she would dress and make herself some tea and toast before going out into the early morning to garden. She loved her garden, and she liked to hear the dawn chorus, she said. Often my husband and I would be woken by the smell of toast wafting up from the kitchen next door. If we looked at the clock, it was always half-past four. 'Poor Mrs Wellington can't sleep,' we would say, and in a few minutes, if we bothered to look, we should see her small figure bent over a flower-bed in the dusky garden.

This went on for several years, and then the old lady died, and a

new, young family moved in next door. But still on summer mornings sometimes, we were woken by the smell of toast, always at half-past four. Our new neighbours laughed to scorn the idea that any of them got up so early in the day, and all of them, they insisted, slept soundly through the night. So strong was the impression that it was old Mrs Wellington that I several times sat up, and peered through the curtains half-expecting to see our old friend bowed over a flower-bed in the shadowy garden. There was never any trace of her, nothing but the faint, first twitters of the dawn chorus . . . and the smell of toast.

Barbara Sleigh

The Carol Singers

Bring out the tall tales now that we told
by the fire as the gas-light bubbled like a diver.
Ghosts whooed like owls in the long nights
when I dared not look over my shoulder; animals
lurked in the cubbyhole under the stairs where the
gas meter ticked. And I remember that we went
singing carols once, when there wasn't the shaving
of a moon to light the flying streets. At the end
of a long road was a drive that led to a large
house, and we stumbled up the darkness of the drive
that night, each one of us afraid, each one holding
a stone in his hand in case, and all of us too brave
to say a word. The wind through the trees
made noises as of old and unpleasant and maybe
web-footed men wheezing in caves. We reached
the black bulk of the house.
'What shall we give them? Hark the Herald?'
'No,' Jack said, 'Good King Wenceslas.
I'll count three.'
One, two, three, and we began to sing,
our voices high and seemingly distant in the
snow-felted darkness round the house that
was occupied by nobody we knew. We stood
close together, near the dark door.
'Good King Wenceslas looked out
On the Feast of Stephen. . .'
And then a small, dry voice, like the voice
of someone who has not spoken for a long time,
joined our singing: a small, dry, egg-shell voice
from the other side of the door: a small, dry voice
through the keyhole. And when we stopped running
we were outside *Our* house; the front room was lovely:
balloons floated under the hot-water-gulping gas;
everything was good again and shone over the town.

'Perhaps it was a ghost,' Jim said,
'Perhaps it was trolls,' Dan said,
who was always reading.

'Let's go in and see if there's any jelly left,'
Jack said. And we did that.

Dylan Thomas

The Legion Marching By

John Mizenas was a remarkable man. I have not seen him for thirty years, but I do not forget him. His children are married and have children of their own, and time has been kind to his beloved Judith. Can one remain the friend of a man whom one has not seen for a generation? I believe it is possible, for I have only to think for a moment, and I can recall his voice, his manner, his laughter, his seriousness; he was a man of spirit and of positive outlook; add to this a long, though now faraway friendship, and I believe that you have sufficient reason — that *I* have sufficient reason — for keeping his memory green.

Think no incautious ill of me when I say that John was ten and I was fourteen when our paths met in interests as diverse as falconry and fishing; we became friends simply because there was no stopping the inclinations of our two natures. His mental equipment was every whit as able as mine, and there was never the feeling of a grudge between us.

It was in the summer of — no, I will not say which summer, because this particular time is so long ago, and the distance — I use the word advisedly — between then and now has a tendency to frighten me. This particular day had been so full of sun and drowsiness and sandwiches and fiercely bright bottles of pop and moorhens and peggy-dishwashers and fish, that we came home in the twilight, half-drugged with all the free favours of nature. I was sleepy as we took our time (that word again!) climbing the cart track from the Dene valley up to the Heastor road; it was all open fields and clumps of bushes in those days, given over entirely to the service of the small, wild creatures that frequented the thick hedges and, from time to time, dared to cross the road which twists down the hill to Heastor village with the great wood on your left, as you come up from the valley.

John was in front of me. Instead of going directly down the road, he crossed over and moved a little to the right, where he leaned on the fence and looked out over the green corn which was losing its colour in the fading light. So I crossed and leaned with him. I didn't speak, because I knew that he was going to find the right words. That was John; a finder and a speaker of the right words.

'Marvellous,' he said. And I just waited.

He pointed. 'Even with the corn near full high, you can still see it.'

I followed his pointing finger. 'Oh, yes. The Roman road.'

He stayed leaning, very still now, as though movement might shatter part of his thought.

'Marvellous,' I said. I did not think it was sycophantic to repeat what he said. It was the right word, after all.

'All those years, Tom. All those years ago.' (I had a tiny inkling of what prompted this.) 'Angles, Saxons, Danes and Normans. Winter cold and summer heat, ploughing and reploughing; century after century. And it's still there.' He used the voice which he naturally used when there was something of magic and mystery in his mind; it had a kind of reverent tone, and it never failed to grip me.

But the grip relaxed, and my next words showed the difference in temperament between us. I said: 'Anything'll last if it's well made.' The accountant's reply to the poet.

We had eaten our sandwiches at about midday, and now my stomach was sending out signals. I was going to suggest that the best thing to do was to get home and see what was for supper, but I didn't. John could indicate an idea with the tiniest inflexion, and I held my tongue.

'The legions,' he said softly, 'Can't you imagine them, Tom?'

I spoke quietly, too. 'I'll let you imagine them. You're better at it than I am.' I knew what was on now. He had mentioned it a few months ago, obliquely, not committing himself, not then.

'The transports, the broad-wheeled supply wagons; their accoutrements, shields, pylums, their leather and bronze, the men at the head carrying the standards. Can't you see them?'

'Can you?'

He smiled. I asked: 'Is it supposed to be tonight, then?'

'Supposed to be?'

'You mean that you believe it and I don't?'

He turned and faced me squarely. 'Let's stay and see them. Now. Tonight is the night. Let's stay!'

'So you do believe it?'

'I'm going to stay and see if I believe it. Once every thirty years, they say, you can see the legion marching north. They pass west of Fenborough, but this stretch, here, is the only place where they can be seen . . .' The words seemed to drift across my mind and fade into the cooling evening. 'Stay, Tom,' he said, and I did not know if it was a request or a command.

I looked into the growing dark, and saw bats, and an owl, and heard little squeaks and scurries. I thought of my mother, getting anxious, but I didn't mention her. I said: 'Yes,' and we climbed the fence, treading almost waist-deep in the border of meadow grass which surrounded the burgeoning wheat. He led, I followed. At length he stopped about five yards from the wall which enclosed the wood, and about the same distance from where the long hump of the road was visible, straight as a sword.

'Let's sit, then,' John said.

We sat. 'I can't see over this grass,' I said.

'You won't have to,' he replied, and it took me a few seconds to see what he meant.

I cannot tell how long we stayed, waiting. The Heastor church clock tolled ten. Men would be coming out of the 'Oak' and the 'Bluebell' and 'The Gordon Arms', at this time. The old clock's announcement was all we heard. There was no traffic at all on the road. It seemed to be an especial kind of stillness.

Faintly, a rumble came to our ears. It was only a train running into Fenborough East station, along the line which shared the valley with the river Dene. Then the fading rumble of the train seemed to blend into a different, more irregular kind of rumble, coming from down the slope and through the woods. My face asked 'Is it?' and John nodded. There was no doubt in his mind and, therefore, I did not doubt either.

The rumbling grew, added a regular rhythm, and an erratic jingle; the wood began to fade, as though it was giving way to day in the midst of night. We could hear the marching feet; John felt, I am sure, how I was feeling, expectant, tense but *delighted* . . .

We saw them.

When I was a boy, I used to enjoy the fine, historical drawings of an artist named Fortunino Matania; I liked the particular way he drew Romans, and I was filled with joy to discover that he was right; the soldiers, marching in the past and showing themselves in a scrap of our present time, were just what I expected, except that they always seemed larger in Matania's pictures, for his Roman women were usually Junoesque and his men six-footers. These men were, on an average, about five-foot five or six, but tough and wiry.

First came the standard bearers, each wearing a tiger skin on head and shoulders, and each carrying a legion's emblem. I was childishly pleased to see the SPQR on the standards, but was puzzled by the fact that they carried two emblems, one of an eagle and the other of a stag's head. Were they two half-legions? I had a feeling that I would never know.

After these two rode the commander, erect, proud, his helmet carrying a brush of green plumes, and then the soldiers, centurions spacing the hundreds. They were marching at ease, talking, and we strained to catch their words. To my ears, if what they spoke was Latin, then it was a very different Latin from the language we learned at school.

John whispered: 'Some of them are Britons. Do you see?'

In our time, it was dark; in theirs was a soft glow of sunshine. I said: 'Are they the group saying words over to each other? That's what it sounds like.'

The soldiers marched in front of us, marched from and into the eternal past. John said: 'I think that some of them are British-born, and they are recruits trying to learn army Latin. That's what the laughter is about.'

Satisfaction and pleasure were in my mind; there was no fear.

Then John scared me. He suddenly stood and shouted: 'Hail Caesar, hail Caesar!' A centurion looked straight at us, and paused for a moment in his step, then turned and marched on. At the end of the column rumbled the baggage wagons, lumbering and broad of wheel. In some of them we saw women; they might have been wives or merely camp-followers. Two, red-haired Britons were in

77

charge of water carts, pulled by donkeys, or mules, I did not know which. Finally came the rear-guard, about fifty men, a junior officer on his horse, and some mounted Britons riding small, thick ponies; these were the scouts but, by the easy way they rode, and by the way in which they kept together, they were not expecting any trouble in this part of the Roman Empire.

Then the light of a day long past filtered away, and left us in our present night. We walked home, not speaking, not even saying 'goodnight' when we parted.

For me, mathematics were and still are childishly easy. I got a good, science degree, and then my accountant's qualifications, and I entered the world of commerce. I loved one woman, who married someone else. Henceforward I was a bachelor, with my own house and a good housekeeper. I kept my love of fishing, and added to that a fair hand at water-colour painting.

John, inevitably, was of nobler stuff. He took classical languages at Oxford, obtained a first class, honours degree, and for his brilliance became a miserably paid schoolmaster. It never bothered him; he could finish a day's work worn out, and the next morning he was refreshed as though by a secret mountain stream. He met Judith when at Oxford; they married, and their children were Rosalind, Juliet and Sebastian, all three as wise as their father and as beautiful as their mother. They seemed ideally happy; how could Judith and her children know that John was willing to forsake them for an insubstantial idea, for a drifting shadow? When he studied in his spare time for a history degree – which he achieved brilliantly, as expected – how could they interpret the signs?

After about twenty-one years, we both returned to Heastor. John was a classics master at an independent school in Fenborough, and I was actuary for and a director of Hewell Engineering, a Fenborough firm with a high reputation. John's wife and kids just about adopted me as an uncle. Perhaps it was because there was a shortage of uncles. I was afraid of my strong attraction to Judith. She was such a prize; any man would have gone overboard for her, and more than once I thought that John did not appreciate her. Had she been mine, I would have made her the heart and centre of my life.

It was a hot summer. Heastor remained as it had always been, no housing estates, just a village in which the most recent building had been done thirty years before. The bosky lanes still led down into the valley of the Dene, and boys of ten and eleven still went fishing. The Roman road was still there, defiant in its green clothing as it ran parallel to the Fenborough road, having ascended the hill by a different and wooded route.

I was in the garden one evening, doing battle with the green-fly on the roses. The gate sounded, and I looked up to see Judith coming across the lawn.

'Hallo Tom.'

'Hallo and welcome,' I said. 'I was just thinking about a pint of cider. Will you join me?'

'That sounds lovely.'

I drew two pints from the barrel in the little dark scullery, and carried them out to the lawn, where Judith had seated herself at the rickety, old table in the corner. She took a long pull at her tankard. 'Isn't it beautiful – a real country drink.'

'I've always thought so,' I said. I put down my tankard. 'How's the family?'

'Fine.'

And I knew at once that all was not fine. The greater the love, the less can truth be dissembled.

She watched an ant walk over the old table top, and then she said: 'Tom, have you – noticed – anything about John, lately?'

I wondered if she knew that, when I came to visit them and she was present, I hardly noticed John. I said: 'What's worrying you, Judith?'

She stared into her tankard, took another long drink and then said: 'There's a barrier.'

I waited.

'There's something on his mind.'

'He's a very intelligent man, and somewhat obsessional. Sometimes his interests take priority. Then, he needs only himself.'

'Yes. He is so intelligent.'

'I would say that you are equally intelligent,' I said, and this was not flattery. She was the wife for John even if she was not always as loved and as appreciated as I thought proper.

'Things were pretty good, until the beginning of this year,' she said. 'Now, there's something changed. I feel that it's something which has been dormant for a long time, and now, here it is. Dormant.'

'The body renews itself every seven years. Does the mind do that too?'

'Dormant.' I could see that the word had a grip on her mind. She repeated it, and seemed to hope that I would go on talking. I did not. After a moment she finished her cider with a swift finality seldom seen in women.

She rose with a smile. 'Thanks for talking, Tom.'

'You've nothing to thank me for.'

'Watch him,' she said, 'and tell me what you think.'

'I can't promise anything. This is intimate ground, this is husband-and-wife stuff. Fools rush in, Judith.'

She smiled. I watched her go. I was not happy.

The next time I visited, John took me aside. He was filled with a dream, an idea. Their children were playing with those of Dr Barnett, whose wife was also visiting.

'Come with me, Tom. I've something to show you.'

So, on that warm, summer evening, we went together down to the smaller of the two sheds at the bottom of the garden. Here, in the musty, dried-earth smell, he unlocked a rough, old chest, made of pine. He took from the chest clothes which seemed to be made of rabbit skins, and thonged sandals, and a rough under-shirt of wide weave, and a large-bladed weapon somewhere between a sword and a machete. He could see that I was puzzled.

His eyes were shining. 'I'd dress in them for you,' he said, 'but someone might come.'

'What's the stuff for? A play?'

He grinned. 'You could say that.'

I just stared at him. I was beginning to remember.

'You and I saw them, as boys, thirty years ago.'

'The legion.'

'Yes.'

My mind raced round all the possibilities, but, as ever, he saw

81

more than I did. 'You're going to –'

'Watch the legion go by. Every thirty years. We know the story.'

'Then, these clothes –'

'Don't you remember, Tom, how I cried "Hail Caesar" – but it was the wrong language? Now if I, clad as a Briton, call to them in their own language, and say that I want to join them . . . don't you see?'

For at least a minute, I was incapable of answering him. I was wondering how this man whom I thought I knew so well had nurtured this idea for thirty years. I did not see what he thought he was achieving. But then, he was the poet, and I was only the accountant.

'John, don't do it.'

'It's just an experiment.'

'Except that you don't know with what you're experimenting. To say the least, it's a very unscientific approach.'

'Thirty years ago tomorrow night?'

'You could be miles out in your calculations –'

'Oh, Tom, you disappoint me! I'm no mathematician, but I worked that out. What do you say – let's both try it!'

He saw by my face that I was set against the idea, and tried with more emotion to stir me into the way he was going. 'Thirty years ago we were kids. Can't we do better, now? . . . Tom, I'm talking about an old friendship.'

'How would you like me to tell Judith about this?'

He smiled, and shook his head. 'You wouldn't do that.'

I knew then what sort of a coward I was. I watched him put the skin clothes and the knife away, and lock the box. He straightened and said: 'You'd never betray a confidence, Tom.' He was expecting a reply; stubborn, I tried not to reply, but I knew that he was right, so at last I said: 'No, I won't tell. But I beg you not to do this.'

All he did was to shake his head, and chuckle.

Less than forty-eight hours later, the police were out looking for John Mizenas. They spread their net wider and wider until at last, inevitably, they decided that he couldn't be found and so they called off the search. The news value diminished until John Mizenas was forgotten by all except a handful of people in Fenborough and Heastor.

I kept my promise, but my mind would not rest. I even feared to meet the possible truth that John Mizenas had met the Romans, and joined them, and had marched with them into the dangerous past, and where, perhaps, with his knowledge of languages, had possibly found a place for his scholarship. As John knew Latin, it would take him about a week to master the sound they gave it, and after that . . .

But this was mere rambling. For me there was the deep personal agony of knowing that Judith and the children regarded me as one of the family. I did not doubt that if, after a respectable interval, I proposed marriage, I would be accepted. I was even sure that in Heastor it would be regarded as a good and happy thing if I married Judith. I was forty-four, she was thirty-three. John was missing, and would later be 'presumed dead'. After that, there was no impediment.

Except that I could not bring myself to believe that John was dead. His ghost did not visit me, I received no supernatural message, but, knowing what I did, I could not bring myself to say the words to Judith.

But if I was not forthcoming, someone else was. Dr Barnett's wife died suddenly, and, a year after, he married Judith, and it was soon a happy case of 'yours, mine and ours' with the increasing family. Now the children of three marriages are grown up, and Judith, in her sixties, is still beautiful, because her mind is open and her spirit is ready for laughter.

I am still a bachelor, not too crusty, I hope, and reasonably sociable. I am over seventy, but I still have something to look forward to.

Come with me, and I will show you.

Here you see a rough suit of skins, and some dateless underwear; good, leather shoes, made by hand, and a cloak, and a sturdy staff. And see how patriarchal I look, having let my beard grow to its present length. Don't I look the part? And when I go up the hill tonight, and wait for them to come as I stand by the old road, I shall have enough knowledge of Latin to speak to them. I shall look for John Mizenas. He may not be there. He may still be forty years old as he was the night he disappeared, or he may be only four years younger than myself. But I must go up there, and wait, and see the legion marching by.

By John Hynam from *The Eighth Ghost Book*

The Haunting of Avenbury Church

Avenbury church? Ah that's haanted all right, I heered un, I heered the organ a-playing and nobody there. Ahd bin to Bromyard to buy a pair of shoes, one Thursday it were, and it were dropping night when I comes to Avenbury. I crossed the stile for the footpath and comes anunt (close by) the church and damn me, I heers the organ playing beautiful, and I tell yer that frit me terrible and I runs all the way to the gate for The Hyde I was that startled.

Well, it come about this way I suppose. There was two brothers lived at Brookhouse, tells me, the one he were a good chap and a used to play the organ in church reg'lar. T'other never did no work and was always a-pothering his brother for money and such. Nobody couldn't suffer un. How it come to happen I don't rightly know, but one evening part they comes to blows on the water bridge over the prill just off the Bromyard road, and the one he kills his brother for dead. And that weren't the end on it, not by no manner of means for arter that the organ used to play nights and no lights nor nobody there. A could hear un on the road and all quiet — there's scores heerd un one time or another.

That come to be the talk of the place, and presently that come on so powerful the passon say he must fall (lay) the ghost, so one day at the same time as the murdering, he comes to the bridge all in his clothes (vestments) and he lights three candles, and he starts to pray, and presently the one candle flickered and went out. The passon he prayed harder but it warn't no good for the second

candle that went out too. Then the passon he prays that hard till the sweat fair run off his nose, and the third candle that started to go down but the passon kept on a-praying and just when it burned blue it started to come up bright again, and just so well it did as if it had a gone out the ghost would ha bested un. That didn't stop the music altogether but the pain had gone out of it and them as lived about there didn't take a lot of notice, but strangers as knowed about it wouldn't go near or nighst the place arter dark, and them as didn't know, well, they got tarrified.

This account is exactly as related to Andrew Haggard of Ledbury about 1925.

Old Madame

Baring-Gould, who was a Church of England clergyman (he wrote the hymn 'Onward Christian Soldiers'), tells a number of ghost stories in his reminiscences. Many of them about an eccentric ancestor known as Old Madame.

A woman who entered the orchard, seeing the trees laden with apples, shook some down and filled her pockets, keeping one in her hand to eat. She turned to the gate into the road, and suddenly there flashed before her in the way the figure of Old Madame in white, pointing to the apple. The poor woman, in an agony of terror, cast it away and fled across the orchard to another exit, a gap, where a slate slab formed a bridge across the stream; but the moment she reached it the figure of the White Lady (another

local name of Old Madame) appeared standing before the bridge, looking at her sternly and pointing to her pocket. It was not till the old goody had emptied it of the stolen apples, that the spectre vanished. This woman I knew: her name was Patience Kite, and she often told me the story, and assured me of its truth.

From *Early Reminiscences* by S. Baring-Gould

Marley's Ghost

One of the most famous, invented, ghost stories is Charles Dickens's *A Christmas Carol*. It all started when the ghost of Jacob Marley, who had been his business partner, appeared to Scrooge, the miserly old man who hated Christmas.

Scrooge lived in chambers which had once belonged to Marley, his deceased partner. They were a gloomy suite of rooms, and the yard was so dark that even Scrooge, who knew its every stone, was fain to grope with his hands. The fog and frost so hung about the black, old gateway of the house, that it seemed as if the Genius of the Weather sat in mournful meditation on the threshold.

Now, it is a fact, that there was nothing at all particular about the knocker on the door, except that it was very large. It is also a fact, that Scrooge had seen it, night and morning, during his whole residence in that place; also that Scrooge had as little of what is called fancy about him as any man in the City of London. Let it also be borne in mind that Scrooge had not bestowed one thought on Marley since he had mentioned his seven years' dead partner that afternoon. And then let any man explain to me, if he can, how it happened that Scrooge, having his key in the lock of the door, saw in the knocker without its undergoing any intermediate process of change: not a knocker, but Marley's face.

Marley's face. It was not in impenetrable shadow as the other objects in the yard were, but had a dismal light about it, like a bad lobster in a dark cellar. It was not angry or ferocious, but looked at Scrooge as Marley used to look: with ghostly spectacles turned up on its ghostly forehead. The hair was curiously stirred, as if by breath or hot air; and, though the eyes were wide open, they were perfectly motionless. That, and its livid colour, made it horrible; but its horror seemed to be in spite of the face and beyond its control, rather than part of its own expression.

As Scrooge looked fixedly at this phenomenon, it was a knocker again.

To say that he was not startled, or that his blood was not conscious of a terrible sensation to which it had been a stranger from infancy, would be untrue. But he put his hand upon the key he had relinquished, turned it sturdily, walked in, and lighted his candle.

He *did* pause, with a moment's irresolution, before he shut the door; and he *did* look cautiously behind it first, as if he half expected to be terrified with the sight of Marley's pigtail sticking out into the hall. But there was nothing on the back of the door, except the screws and nuts that held the knocker on; so he said, 'Pooh, pooh!' and closed it with a bang.

The sound resounded through the house like thunder. Every room above, and every cask in the wine-merchant's cellars below, appeared to have a separate peal of echoes of its own. Scrooge was not a man to be frightened by echoes. He fastened the door, and walked across the hall, and up the stairs: slowly too: trimming the candle as he went.

Up Scrooge went. Darkness is cheap, and Scrooge liked it. But before he shut his heavy door, he walked through his rooms to see that all was right. He had just enough recollection of the face to desire to do that.

Sitting-room, bedroom, lumber-room. All as they should be. Nobody under the table, nobody under the sofa; a small fire in the grate; spoon and basin ready; and the little saucepan of gruel (Scrooge had a cold in his head) upon the hob. Nobody under the bed; nobody in the closet; nobody in his dressing-gown, which was hanging up in a suspicious attitude against the wall.

Quite satisfied, he closed his door, and locked himself in; double-locked himself in, which was not his custom. Thus secured against surprise, he took off his cravat; put on his dressing-gown and slippers, and his night-cap; and sat down before the fire to take his gruel.

It was a very low fire indeed; nothing on such a bitter night. He was obliged to sit close to it, and brood over it, before he could extract the least sensation of warmth from such a handful of fuel. The fireplace was an old one, built by some Dutch merchant long ago, and paved all round with quaint Dutch tiles, designed to illustrate the Scriptures. Hundreds of figures, to attract his thoughts; and yet that face of Marley, seven years dead, came like the ancient Prophet's rod, and swallowed up the whole. If each smooth tile had been a blank at first, with power to shape some picture on its surface from the disjointed fragments of his thoughts, there would have been a copy of old Marley's head on every one.

'Humbug!' said Scrooge; and walked across the room.

After several turns, he sat down again. As he threw his head back in the chair, his glance happened to rest upon a bell, a disused bell, that hung in the room, and communicated for some purpose now forgotten with a chamber, in the highest storey of the building. It was with great astonishment, and with a strange, inexplicable dread, that as he looked, he saw this bell begin to swing. It swung so softly in the outset that it scarcely made a sound; but soon it rang out loudly, and so did every bell in the house.

It might have lasted half a minute, or a minute, but it seemed an hour. The bells ceased as they had begun, together. They were succeeded by a clanking noise, deep down below; as if some person were dragging a heavy chain over the casks in the wine-merchant's cellar. Scrooge then remembered to have heard that ghosts in haunted houses were described as dragging chains.

The cellar door flew open with a booming sound, and then he heard the noise much louder, on the floors below; then coming up the stairs; then coming straight towards his door.

'It's humbug still!' said Scrooge. 'I won't believe it.'

His colour changed though, when, without a pause, it came on through the heavy door, and passed into the room before his eyes. Upon its coming in, the dying flame leaped up, as though it cried, 'I know him! Marley's Ghost!' and fell again.

The same face: the very same. Marley in his pigtail, usual waistcoat, tights and boots; the tassels on the latter bristling, like his pigtail, and his coat skirts, and the hair upon his head. The chain he drew was clasped about his middle. It was long, and wound about him like a tail; and it was made (for Scrooge observed it closely) of cash-boxes, keys, padlocks, ledgers, deeds, and heavy purses wrought in steel. His body was transparent; so that Scrooge, observing him, and looking through his waistcoat, could see the two buttons on his coat behind.

Scrooge had often heard it said that Marley had no bowels, but he had never believed it until now.

No, nor did he believe it even now. Though he looked the phantom through and through, and saw it standing before him; though he felt the chilling influence of its death-cold eyes; and marked the very texture of the folded kerchief bound about its head and chin, which wrapper he had not observed before: he was still incredulous, and fought against his senses.

'How now!' said Scrooge, caustic and cold as ever. 'What do you want with me?'

'Much!' – Marley's voice, no doubt about it.

'Who are you?'

'Ask me who I *was*.'

'Who *were* you then?' said Scrooge, raising his voice. 'You're particular – for a shade.' He was going to say '*to* a shade', but substituted this, as more appropriate.

'In life I was your partner, Jacob Marley.'

'Can you – can you sit down?' asked Scrooge, looking doubtfully at him.

'I can.'

'Do it then.'

Scrooge had asked the question, because he didn't know whether a ghost so transparent might find himself in a condition to take a chair; and felt that in the event of its being impossible, it might involve the necessity of an embarrassing explanation. But the Ghost sat down on the opposite side of the fireplace, as if he were quite used to it.

'You don't believe in me,' observed the Ghost.

'I don't,' said Scrooge.

'What evidence would you have of my reality beyond that of your senses?'

'I don't know,' said Scrooge.

'Why do you doubt your senses?'

'Because,' said Scrooge, 'a little thing affects them. A slight disorder of the stomach makes them cheats. You may be an undigested bit of beef, a blot of mustard, a crumb of cheese, a fragment of an underdone potato. There's more of gravy than of grave about you, whatever you are!'

Scrooge was not much in the habit of cracking jokes, nor did he feel, in his heart, by any means waggish then. The truth is, that he tried to be smart, as a means of distracting his own attention, and keeping down his terror; for the Spectre's voice disturbed the very marrow of his bones.

'All humbug, I tell you – humbug!'

At this the Spirit raised a frightful cry, and shook its chain with such a dismal and appalling noise that Scrooge held on tight to his chair, to save himself from falling in a swoon. But how much greater was his horror, when the Phantom taking off the bandage round its head, as if it were too warm to wear indoors, its lower jaw dropped down upon its breast!

Scrooge fell upon his knees and clasped his hands before his face.

'Mercy!' he said. 'Dreadful apparition, why do you trouble me?'

'Man of worldly mind!' replied the Ghost, 'do you believe in me or not?'

'I do,' said Scrooge. 'I must. But why do spirits walk the earth, and why do they come to me?'

'It is required of every man,' the Ghost returned, 'that the spirit within him should walk abroad among his fellow men, and travel far and wide; and if that spirit goes not forth in life, it is condemned to do so after death. It is doomed to wander through the world – oh, woe is me! – and witness what it cannot share, but might have shared on earth, and turned to happiness!'

Again the Spectre raised a cry, and shook its chain, and wrung its shadowy hands.

'You are fettered,' said Scrooge, trembling. 'Tell me why?'

'I wear the chain I forged in life,' replied the Ghost. 'I made it link by link, and yard by yard; I girded it on of my own free will, and of my own free will I wore it. Is its pattern strange to *you*?'

Scrooge trembled more and more.

'Or would you know,' pursued the Ghost, 'the weight and length of the strong coil you bear yourself? It was full as heavy and as long as this, seven Christmas Eves ago. You have laboured on it, since. It is a ponderous chain!'

Scrooge glanced about him on the floor, in the expectation of finding himself surrounded by some fifty or sixty fathoms of iron cable: but he could see nothing.

'Jacob,' he said imploringly. 'Old Jacob Marley, tell me more. Speak comfort to me, Jacob.'

'I have none to give,' the Ghost replied. 'It comes from other regions, Ebenezer Scrooge, and is conveyed by other ministers, to other kinds of men. Nor can I tell you what I would. A very little more, is all permitted to me. I cannot rest, I cannot stay, I cannot linger anywhere. My spirit never walked beyond our counting-house – mark me! – in life my spirit never roved beyond the

93

narrow limits of our money-changing hole; and weary journeys lie before me!'

'You must have been very slow about it, Jacob,' Scrooge observed, in a business-like manner, though with humility and deference.

'Slow!' the Ghost repeated.

'Seven years dead,' mused Scrooge. 'And travelling all the time!'

'The whole time,' said the Ghost. 'No rest, no peace. Incessant torture of remorse.'

'You travel fast?' said Scrooge.

'On the wings of the wind,' replied the Ghost.

'You might have got over a great quantity of ground in seven years,' said Scrooge.

The Ghost, on hearing this, set up another cry.

'Oh, captive, bound, and double-ironed,' cried the Phantom, 'not to know that any Christian spirit working kindly in its little sphere, whatever it may be, will find its mortal life too short for its vast means of usefulness. Not to know that no space of regret can make amends for one life's opportunity misused! Yet such was I! Oh! Such was I!'

'But you were always a good man of business, Jacob,' faltered Scrooge, who now began to apply this to himself.

'Business!' cried the Ghost, wringing its hands again. 'Mankind was my business. The common welfare was my business; charity, mercy, forbearance, and benevolence, were, all, my business. The dealings of my trade were but a drop of water in the comprehensive ocean of my business!'

It held up its chain at arm's length, as if that were the cause of all its unavailing grief, and flung it heavily upon the ground again.

'At this time of the rolling year,' the Spectre said, 'I suffer most. Why did I walk through crowds of fellow beings with my eyes turned down, and never raise them to that blessed Star which led the Wise Men to a poor abode! Were there no poor homes to which its light would have conducted *me*!'

Scrooge was very much dismayed to hear the Spectre going on at this rate, and began to quake exceedingly.

'Hear me!' cried the Ghost. 'My time is nearly gone.'

'I will,' said Scrooge. 'But don't be hard upon me! Don't be flowery, Jacob! Pray!'

'How it is that I appear before you in a shape that you can see, I may not tell. I have sat invisible beside you many and many a day.'

It was not an agreeable idea. Scrooge shivered, and wiped the perspiration from his brow.

'That is no light part of my penance,' pursued the Ghost. 'I am here tonight to warn you, that you have yet a chance and hope of escaping my fate. A chance and hope of my procuring, Ebenezer.'

'You were always a good friend to me,' said Scrooge. 'Thank 'ee!'

'You will be haunted,' resumed the Ghost, 'by Three Spirits.'

Scrooge's countenance fell almost as low as the Ghost's had done.

'Is that the chance and hope you mentioned, Jacob?' he demanded in a faltering voice.

'It is.'

'I – I think I'd rather not,' said Scrooge.

'Without their visits,' said the Ghost, 'you cannot hope to shun the path I tread. Expect the first tomorrow, when the bell tolls one.'

'Couldn't I take 'em all at once, and have it over, Jacob?' hinted Scrooge.

'Expect the second on the next night at the same hour. The third upon the next night when the last stroke of twelve has ceased to vibrate. Look to see me no more; and look that, for your own sake, you remember what has passed between us!'

When it had said these words, the Spectre took its wrapper from the table, and bound it round its head, as before. Scrooge knew this, by the smart sound its teeth made, when the jaws were brought together by the bandage. He ventured to raise his eyes again, and found his supernatural visitor confronting him in an erect attitude, with its chain wound over and about its arm.

The apparition walked backward from him; and at every step it took, the window raised itself a little, so that when the Spectre reached it, it was wide open. It beckoned Scrooge to approach, which he did. When they were within two paces of each other, Marley's Ghost held up its hand, warning him to come no nearer. Scrooge stopped.

Not so much in obedience, as in surprise and fear; for on the raising of the hand, he became sensible of confused noises in the air; incoherent sounds of lamentation and regret; wailings inexpressibly sorrowful and self-accusatory. The Spectre, after listening for a moment, joined in the mournful dirge; and floated out upon the bleak, dark night.

Scrooge followed to the window: desperate in his curiosity. He looked out.

The air was filled with phantoms, wandering hither and thither in restless haste, and moaning as they went. Every one of them wore chains like Marley's Ghost; some few (they might be guilty governments) were linked together; none were free. Many had been personally known to Scrooge in their lives. He had been quite familiar with one old ghost, in a white waistcoat, with a monstrous, iron safe attached to its ankle, who cried piteously at being unable to assist a wretched woman with an infant, whom it saw below, upon a doorstep. The misery in them all was, clearly, that they sought to interfere, for good, in human matters, and had lost the power for ever.

Whether these creatures faded into mist, or mist enshrouded them, he could not tell. But they and their spirit voices faded together; and the night became as it had been when he walked home.

Scrooge closed the window, and examined the door by which the Ghost had entered. It was double-locked, as he had locked it with his own hands, and the bolts were undisturbed. He tried to say 'Humbug!' but stopped at the first syllable. And being, from the emotion he had undergone, or the fatigues of the day, or his glimpse of the Invisible World, or the dull conversation with the Ghost, or the lateness of the hour, much in need of repose; went straight to bed, without undressing, and fell asleep upon the instant.

From *A Christmas Carol* by Charles Dickens

Dreams

The Golden Bough

In his book *The Golden Bough*, Sir James Frazer tells of some curious early theories about dreams and dreamers.

The soul of a sleeper is supposed (among certain primitive people) to wander away from his body and actually to visit the places, to see the persons, and to perform the acts of which he dreams. For example, when an Indian of Brazil or Guiana wakes up from a sound sleep, he is firmly convinced that his soul has been away hunting, fishing, or felling trees, or whatever else he had dreamed of doing, while all the time his body has been lying motionless in his hammock . . .

Now the absence of the soul in sleep has its dangers, for if for any

cause the soul should be permanently detained away from the body, the person thus deprived of the vital principle must die. There is a German belief that the soul escapes from the sleeper's mouth in the form of a white mouse, or a little bird, and that to prevent the return of the bird or animal would be fatal to the sleeper. Hence in Transylvania, they say that you should not let a child sleep with its mouth open, or its soul will slip out in the shape of a mouse, and the child will never wake . . .

Still more dangerous is it, in the opinion of primitive man, to move a sleeper or alter his appearance, for if this were done the soul on its return might not be able to find or recognise its body, and so the person would die.

From *The Golden Bough* by Sir James George Frazer

The Pedlar's Dream

One of the odd things about dreams is that sometimes they do come true. I don't mean the kind of dreams that people sing about, but the real ones you have when you are fast asleep.

Here are accounts of three such dreams. The first is an old English folk tale in which good luck is brought to the dreamer, and the last two are dreams giving warnings. One happened at the beginning of this century, but the last took place thousands of years ago.

In the village of Swaffham in Norfolk there once lived a pedlar, in a small, tumble-down cottage, for he made very little money by going from door to door, his dog at his heels, selling ribbons, pins and bits and bobs to the women of the neighbouring villages.

One hot, summer evening he had knocked at I don't know how many doors, without selling so much as a thimble. When at last he reached home again, he sat himself down in the shade of the little hawthorn tree that grew in his scrap of a garden, and I don't know which was the more thankful to take the weight off his feet, the pedlar or his dog. In no time at all they were both fast asleep.

While the pedlar slept, in a dream he seemed to hear a voice saying: 'Go to London Bridge, and there you will hear some wonderfully good news.'

When he woke he said to his dog with a yawn:

'London Bridge is it, Towser? You won't catch me walking the boots off my feet for a bit of a dream. I've better use for my shoe leather than that!' – for London Bridge was more than 90 miles away – and the dog thumped his tail as if he agreed.

The following evening, the pedlar was so tired when he got home that he fell asleep in his chair by the fire, for this time the day had been cold and wet, and bless me if he didn't dream the same dream again. And on the third night too, snug in bed, with the blankets pulled round his ears, he dreamed exactly the same dream all over again.

'Go to London Bridge and there you will hear some wonderfully good news!' said the voice.

So thinking that three times are lucky, the pedlar put on his boots, locked up his house, and, with his dog trotting beside him, set off for London.

When at last he reached London Bridge, he wandered up and down, admiring the fine shops and houses that lined it on either side in those far-off days, and the ships sailing on the sparkling river. But of all the hurrying crowds not a soul spoke to him, let alone told him any good news. At the end of the second day spent wandering up and down, he said to his dog:

'It's my opinion that we've come on a fool's errand, Towser, my boy. But there were three dreams, so we'll give it three days. If nothing happens tomorrow, back we'll go to Swaffham!'

At the end of the third day a baker came out of one of the shops the pedlar had passed so often and said angrily:

'Three days I've watched you pacing up and down outside my shop! You'll wear down the stones of London Bridge if you go on like this. Haven't you something better to do? It's my opinion you're up to no good!'

'I'm as honest a man as you, I dare say,' said the pedlar, who had never cheated anyone from so much as a needle-full of thread. 'I'm here because on three nights running, I dreamed that a voice said to

100

me: "Go to London Bridge and then you'll hear some wonderfully good news." But to tell the truth, you're the first person to speak to me.'

'Dreams is it!' exploded the baker. 'You crazy fellow! You aren't the only one to have 'em. Why, only last night I had one myself. I dreamed that a voice said to me: "Go to the village of Swaffham and dig beneath the hawthorn tree and there in a scrap of a garden, you'll find a wonderful treasure!" Well, do you suppose I'd be such a fool as to . . . Hi! Where are you going? Come back!'

But the pedlar was already out of earshot. He was on his way back to Swaffham twice as fast as he left it, with his dog running behind him. When at last he reached his cottage, he dug down under the hawthorn tree in his scrap of a garden, and there he found the most wonderful treasure.

If you don't believe this story, go to Swaffham church, and there you will see the figure of the pedlar, with his pack on his back and his dog beside him, carved in gratitude, for part of his treasure he spent in building up this very church.

An Old English Legend, retold by Barbara Sleigh

The Duke of Portland's Dream

The Duke of Portland's dream before the Coronation of King Edward VII was so practical that there can be little doubt that his account of it was true.

'The most important ceremony in which I was officially concerned was the Coronation of King Edward (VII). By this time all the Departments of State were thoroughly accustomed to large ceremonies . . . and as they received long notice through the postponement of the ceremony until the Autumn owing to the serious illness of HM, everything was more or less easy and eventually went off without a hitch.

'Before the Coronation I had a remarkable dream. The State Coach had to pass through the Arch at the Horse Guards on the way to Westminster Abbey. I dreamed that it stuck in the Arch, and that some of the Life Guards on duty were compelled to hew off the crown upon the coach before it could be freed. When I told the Crown Equerry, Colonel Ewart, he laughed and said "What do dreams matter?" "At all events," I replied, "let us have the coach and arch measured." So this was done, and to my astonishment we found that the Arch was nearly two feet too low to allow the coach to pass through. I returned to Colonel Ewart in triumph, and said, "What do you think of dreams now?" "I think it's damned fortunate you had one," he replied.

'It appears that the State Coach had not been driven through the arch for some time, and that the level of the road had since been raised during repairs. So I am not sorry that my dinner disagreed with me that night; and I only wish all nightmares were as useful.'

William Cavendish-Bentinck, Duke of Portland

Pharaoh's Dream

Pharaoh, King of Egypt, had a dream, and when morning came he was troubled in his mind, so that he summoned all the magicians and sages of Egypt. He told them his dream, but there was no one who could interpret it for him. Then Pharaoh's chief butler spoke up and said:

'Once Pharaoh was angry with his servants, and he imprisoned me and the chief baker in the house of the captain of the guard. One night we both dreamed dreams, each needing its own interpretation. We had with us a young Hebrew, named Joseph, a slave of the captain of the guard, and we told him our dreams and he interpreted them for us, and each dream came true as it had been interpreted. I was restored to my position, and the baker was hanged.'

Pharaoh thereupon sent for Joseph, and they hurriedly brought him out of the dungeon. He shaved and changed his clothes, and came in to Pharaoh. Pharaoh said to him:

'I have heard it said that you can understand and interpret dreams.'

Joseph answered:

'Not I, but God.'

Then Pharaoh said to Joseph:

'This was my dream. I was standing on the bank of the Nile, and there came up out of the river seven cows, fat and sleek, and they grazed on the reeds. After them seven other cows came up that were poor, very gaunt and lean; I have never seen such gaunt creatures in all Egypt. These lean, gaunt cows devoured the first cows, the fat ones. They were swallowed up, but no one could have guessed that they were in the bellies of the others, which looked as gaunt as before. Then I woke up, and after I had fallen asleep again, I saw in another dream seven ears of corn, full and ripe, growing on one stalk. Growing up after them were seven other ears, shrivelled, thin, and blighted by the east wind, and the thin ears swallowed up the seven ripe ears. When I woke and told all this to the magicians, no one could explain it to me.'

Joseph said: 'Pharaoh's dreams are one dream. God has told Pharaoh what he will do. The seven fine cows and the seven ears of corn are seven good years; and the seven lean and gaunt cows that came up after them, are seven bad years; and the empty ears of corn blighted by the east wind will be seven years of famine. It is as I have said to Pharaoh. There will be seven years of great plenty throughout the land. After them will come seven years of famine. All the years of plenty will be forgotten, and the famine will bring ruin to the land. This is what Pharaoh should do. He should appoint controllers over the land and take one-fifth of the grain of Egypt during the seven years of plenty, and keep it under guard against the seven years of famine which will come upon Egypt.'

The plan pleased Pharaoh, and he said:

'Can we find a man like this man; one who has the spirit of a god in him?'

And he said to Joseph: 'You shall be in charge of my household.

Only my royal throne shall make me greater than you shall be!'

And he took off his signet-ring and put it on Joseph's finger; he had him dressed in fine linen; and hung a gold chain round his neck. He mounted him on his chariot, and men cried 'Make way!' before him.

During the seven years of plenty there were abundant harvests, and Joseph gathered a fifth of the wheat produced in those years and stored it in the cities, and it was beyond all measure, like the sands of the sea.

When the seven years of plenty in Egypt came to an end, began seven years of famine as Joseph had foretold. So when the famine spread through all Egypt, the people cried to Pharaoh for bread, and he ordered them to go to Joseph and do as he told them. And Joseph opened the granaries and sold corn to the Egyptians. The whole world came to Egypt to buy corn from Joseph, so severe was the famine everywhere.

Adapted from 'The Book of Genesis' from the *New English Bible*

Strange Remedies

Curses

Early remedies were often based on a mixture of common sense and magic. Some of these might be thought almost worse than the complaint, but they are all genuine, old country cures.

A Remedy for the Plague
Among the excellent and approved medecines for the Pestilence there is none worthy and avaylable when the sore appeareth. Then take a Cock Pullet and pluck of the feathers of the taile or hinder part till the rump be bare, then hold the bare of the said Pullet to the sore and the Pullet will gape and labour for life and in the end he die then take another Pullet and doe the like and so another as the Pullets doe die, for when the Poison is Drawn out the last Pullet that is offered thereto will live. The sore presently is assuaged and the Party recovereth.

From *A Butler's Recipe Book*, 1719

A Remedy for Fits
Fry some mice whole and eat them. Or eat a page of the Bible put between bread and butter. The liver of forty frogs dried and prepared has also been found beneficial.

A Remedy for Shingles
Scrape verdigris from the Church Bell and apply as an ointment.

A Remedy for Very Many Ills
Spiders rolled in butter and eaten.

A Remedy for Whooping Cough

Eat of bread that was baked on Good Friday. This will keep for seven years.

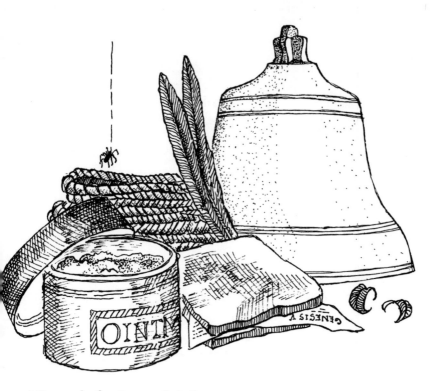

A Remedy for Stomach Ache

If the pain be desperate, tie a rope round the feet and hang upside down from the rafters. This is said to undo the knots in the guts.

Goblin Ointment

Old Mother Margery made her living by nursing the sick and minding babies. She was as kind and simple an old soul as you'd be likely to meet in a month of Sundays.

One night, she heard such a banging at the door as though the king himself wanted to come in. She ran at once to see who was making such a racket, and there, standing on the door-step, was nothing more than a queer, ragged, little fellow who could not so much as reach the door knocker. She didn't much like the look of him, with his wispy hair, and green, squinty eyes, but when he asked her to come and mind his baby, because his missus was too sick to look after it, she thought to herself 'Poor dear thing!' and threw her shawl over her head and followed him outside. To her surprise, waiting there was a great black horse.

'Well, jump up woman!' said the little man as he mounted. Old Margery didn't like the look of the creature, with its stamping hooves and glaring, red eyes, any more than its master. But she thought of the poor, sick mother – and perhaps of the silver pieces she had been promised – and heaved herself up behind the little man, and they were off, so fast that she shut her eyes tight, which was why she could never remember the direction they had taken.

At last they stopped outside the door of a tumble-down cottage, Old Margery half dead with fright at the speed of their going. In they went, and there was the poor, sick mother, with nothing but a few, old sacks thrown over her, and a bundle of rags for a pillow, and the rain dripping through a hole in the roof.

'Poor thing! Poor, pretty thing!' said Margery to herself, and she picked up the baby, who was lying beside its mother, and rocked him on her knee. He was a poor, skinny, little thing. 'What else could you expect?' said Margery to herself, looking about her at the tumble-down room. 'But I've never before seen a child with little points to his ears, sharp enough to prick your fingers!'

Now the young mother was moving restlessly on her ragged bed, and presently she took from under her pillow a little box of ointment.

'As soon as the baby is wide awake and opens his eyes,' she said to Margery, 'Be sure and smear the ointment on his eye-lids.'

Well, this was a thing she had never been asked to do before, but she did as she was told. The baby soon began to whimper and to open his eyes. She just had time to notice that they were as squinty as his father's, before she smeared on the ointment – and at once the whimpering changed to smiles and gurgles of delight.

'Well, that's as strange a way of stopping a baby's tears as ever I met with!' said Old Margery to herself, and, when no one was looking, she smeared some ointment on one of her own eyelids. At once, all around her was changed. The rags and the tatters were gone. The sick woman was lying on a silken couch, covered with soft, embroidered rugs. The tumble-down cottage room had

become large and grandly furnished, with golden mirrors hanging on the panelled walls, and silver, brocaded curtains at the windows. Even the door-knobs were made of lumps of crystal as big as gob-stoppers. As for the baby, he was now as big and bonny a little fellow as Margery had ever dandled, for all his squinty eyes and pointy ears. She nearly dropped him in surprise.

'Mercy on us!' said Old Margery to herself. 'If I haven't got among goblin people! But least said soonest mended. I'd best keep mum as a turnip about it. It's as much as my life is worth to let them know I've found their secret out!' So she kept her peace.

When the sick woman was well enough, Old Margery bobbed a curtsey to the little man, put her silver pieces in her pocket, and was off home as fast as her legs would carry her.

Next day, off she went to market to spend her silver pieces, and who should she see there but the little man with the squinty eyes, doddling from stall to stall, helping himself to whatever he fancied, and pushing it all in a great, bulging sack; and paying no one so much as a penny piece! The strange thing was that nobody seemed to notice.

When he came to the stall where Old Margery was choosing something tasty for her supper, she dropped a curtsey and said:

'And how is your honour this fine day? And I hope the pretty lady and the dear, little baby are well?'

The little man started so violently when he heard her that he nearly upset his bulging sack.

'Woman!' he said, and his squinty eyes flashed green with anger, 'Do you mean to tell me that you can see me today? You interfering, old varmint!'

'See you?' says Margery, none too pleased at being called an old varmint, 'to be sure I can see you, *and* what you're up to with your great, bulging sack!'

'Then you must have used the ointment on your own eyes!' said the little man.

'Why so I did,' said Margery, beginning to feel a bit put out that she had been discovered. 'But only on my right eye, to be sure, your honour.'

'Then, woman,' says he, 'you'll see no more with it! Take that!'

And there and then, he fetched her such a blow in her right eye that it made her cry out.

'What's the matter, mother?' asked the stall-keeper.

'My eye, my eye!' said Margery. 'You saw yourself how the little man hit me!'

'What little man?' said the stall-keeper in surprise. 'I've seen no little man here. There's been no one near my stall since noon except yourself, more's the pity!'

True enough the little fellow had vanished, and, what was worse, so had the silver piece from her purse, *and* the sight of her right eye, for she never saw hide nor hair with it again.

An Old English Folk Tale, retold by Barbara Sleigh.

The Split Dog

Had me a little dog once was the best rabbit dog you ever saw. Well, he was runnin' a rabbit one day, and some fool had left a scythe lying in the grass with the blade straight up. That poor, little dog ran smack into it and it split him open from the tip of his nose right straight on down his tail.

Well I saw him fall apart and I ran and slapped him back together. I had jerked off my shirt, so I wrapped him up in that right quick and ran to the house. Set him in a box and poured turpentine all over the shirt. I kept him near the stove. Set him out in the sun part of the time. Oh, I could see him still breathin' a little, and I hoped I wouldn't lose him. And after about three weeks I could see him try to wiggle now and then. Let him stay bandaged another three weeks – and then one morning I heard him bark. So I started unwrappin' him, and in a few minutes out he jumped, spry as ever.

But, – don't you know! – in my excitement blame if I hadn't put him together wrong way-to. He had two legs up and two legs down.

Anyhow, it turned out he was twice as good a rabbit dog after that. He'd run on two legs till he got tired, and then flip over and just keep right on.

Ah Lord! That little dog could run comin' and goin' and bark at both ends.

'A North Caroline Story.' From *Scenes and Characters* by Skitt, 1859

Francis Kilvert's Diary

To call down a curse on someone is surely a form of witchcraft – if it works. There are many tales of curses that seem to have succeeded. The Reverend Francis Kilvert tells the story of one in his diary which seems to have been completely successful.

The Reverend Francis Kilvert wrote in his diary on Thursday 8 December 1870:

Near capel y fin at the mouth of the dingle on the mountainside

stood the house of Ty yr deol (the house of vengeance). Some crime had been perpetuated on the spot and the place was accursed. When the workmen were building the house they heard a voice which seemed to fall from the air and come down the dingle, saying 'Move the work across the green.' 'For why?' called back the astonished workmen. 'The spot is accursed,' said the voice solemnly. 'For how long?' shouted the workmen. 'Until the ninth generation,' returned the voice. Three attempts were made to build the house. Twice the house fell. The third time the house was built. One night in winter a young man came up the mountain to court his sweetheart, who lived in the Ty yr deol, the accursed, ill-fated house. His greyhound whined at the door, and hung back and refused to enter the house, and no coaxing would induce him to come in. The young man took it as a warning and returned home. That night there was a land slip, or a sudden mass of snow melted down the dingle driving the ice and water before it. The accursed house was overwhelmed and swept away and everyone in the house perished.

Inscription on a Market Cross

On the market cross at Devizes was inscribed this account of a woman who called down a curse on her own head.

On Thursday, the 25th January 1753, Ruth Pierce, of Potterne in this county, agreed with three other women to buy a sack of wheat in the market, each paying her due proportion towards the same. One of these women, in collecting the several quarters of money, discovered a deficiency, and demanded of Ruth Pierce the sum which was wanting to make good the amount. Ruth Pierce protested that she had paid her share, and said that she might wish she should drop dead if she had not. She rashly repeated this awful wish, when, to the consternation of the surrounding multitude, she instantly fell down and expired, having the money concealed in her hand.

Yallery Brown

Once upon a time, and a very good time it was, though it wasn't in my time, nor in your time, nor any one else's time, there was a young lad of eighteen or so named Tom Tiver working on the Hall Farm. One Sunday he was walking across the west field. 'Twas a beautiful, July night, warm and still and the air was full of little sounds as though the trees and grass were chattering to themselves. And all at once there came a bit ahead of him the pitifullest greetings he ever heard, sob-sobbing, like a bairn spent with fear, and nigh heart-broken; breaking off into a moan and then rising again in a long, whimpering wailing that made him feel sick to hark to it. He began to look everywhere for the poor creature. 'It must be Sally Bratton's child,' he thought to himself; 'she was always a flighty thing, and never looked after it. Like as not, she's flaunting about the lanes, and has clean forgot the babby.' But though he looked and looked, he could see nought. And presently the whimpering got louder and stronger in the quietness, and he thought he could make out words of some sort. He hearkened with all his ears, and the sorry thing was saying words all mixed up with sobbing – 'Ooh! the stone, the great, big stone! ooh! the stone on top!'

Naturally he wondered where the stone might be, and he looked again, and there by the hedge bottom was a great, flat stone, nigh buried in the mools, and hid in the cotted grass and weeds. One of the stones was called the 'Strangers' Tables'. However, down he fell on his knee-bones by that stone, and harkened again. Clearer than ever, but tired and spent with greeting came the little, sobbing voice – 'Ooh! ooh! the stone, the stone on top.' He was gey, and misliking to meddle with the thing, but he couldn't stand the whimpering babby, and he tore like mad at the stone, till he felt it lifting from the mools, and all at once it came with a sough out o' the damp earth and the tangled grass and growing things. And there in the hole lay a tiddy thing on its back, blinking up at the moon and at him. 'Twas no bigger than a year-old babby, but it had long, cotted hair and beard, twisted round and round its body so that you couldn't see its clothes; and the hair was all yaller and shining and silky, like a bairn's; but the face of it was old and as if 'twere hundreds of years since 'twas young and smooth. Just a heap of wrinkles, and two bright, black eyne in the midst, set in a lot of shining, yaller hair; and the skin was the colour of the fresh-turned earth in the spring – brown as brown could be, and its bare hands and feet were brown like the face of it. The greeting had stopped, but the tears were standing on its cheek, and the tiddy thing looked mazed-like in the moonshine and the night air.

The creature's eyne got used-like to the moonlight, and presently he looked up in Tom's face as bold as ever was; 'Tom,' says he, 'thou'rt a good lad!' as cool as thou can think, says he, 'Tom, thou'rt a good lad!' and his voice was soft and high and piping like a little bird twittering.

Tom touched his hat, and began to think what he ought to say: 'Houts!' says the thing again, 'thou needn't be feared o' me; thou'st done me a better turn than thou know'st, my lad, and I'll do as much for thee!' Tom couldn't speak yet, but he thought, 'Lord! for sure 'tis a bogle!'

'No!' says he as quick as quick, 'I am no bogle, but ye'd best not ask me what I be; anyways I be a good friend o' thine.' Tom's very knee-bones struck, for certainly an ordinary body couldn't have known what he'd been thinking to himself, but he looked so kind-like, and spoke so fair, that he made bold to get out, a bit quavery-like –

'Might I be axing to know your honour's name?'

'H'm,' says he, pulling his beard; 'as for that' – and he thought a bit – 'ay so,' he went on at 'tis 'Yallery Brown thou mayst call me, Yallery Brown; 'tis my nature see'st thou, and as for a name 'twill do as any other. Yallery Brown, Tom, Yallery Brown's thy friend, my lad.'

'Thankee, master,' says Tom, quite meek-like.

'And now,' he says, 'I'm in a hurry tonight, but tell me quick, what'll I do for thee? Wilt have a wife? I can give thee the finest lass in town. Wilt be rich? I'll give thee gold as much as thou can carry. Or wilt have help wi' thy work? Only say the word.'

Tom scratched his head. 'Well, as for a wife, I have no hanker-ing after such; they're but bothersome bodies, and I have women-folk at home as'll mend my clouts; and for gold that's as may be, but for work there, I can't abide work, and if thou'lt give me a helpin' hand in it I'll thank —'

'Stop,' says he, quick as lightning, 'I'll help thee and welcome, but if ever thou sayest that to me — if ever thou thankest me, see'st thou, thou'lt never see me more. Mind that now; I want no thanks, I'll have no thanks'; and he stampt his tiddy foot on the earth and looked as wicked as a raging bull.

'Mind that now, great lump that thou be,' he went on, calming down a bit, 'and if ever thou need'st help, or get'st into trouble, call on me and just say, "Yallery Brown, come from the mools, I want thee!" and I'll be wi' thee at once; and now,' says he, picking a dandelion puff, 'good night to thee,' and he blowed it up, and it all came into Tom's eyne and ears. Soon as Tom could see again the tiddy creature was gone, and but for the stone on end and the hole at his feet, he'd have thought he'd been dreaming.

Well, Tom went home and to bed; and by the morning he'd nigh forgot all about it. But when he went to the work, there was none to do! All was done already: the horses seen to; the stables cleaned out; everything in its proper place; and he'd nothing to do but sit with his hands in his pockets. And so it went on day after day, all the work done by Yallery Brown, and better done, too, than he could have done it himself. And if the master gave him more work, he sat down, and the work did itself, the singeing irons, or the broom, or what not, set to, and with ne'er a hand put to it, would get through in no time. For he never saw Yallery Brown in daylight; only in the darkling he saw him hopping about, like a will-o-th'-wyke without his lanthorn.

At first, 'twas mighty fine for Tom; he'd nought to do and good pay for it; but by-and-by, things began to go vicey-varsy. If the work was done for Tom, 'twas undone for the other lads; if his buckets were filled, theirs were upset; if his tools were sharpened, theirs were blunted and spoiled; if his horses were clean as daisies, theirs were splashed with muck and so on: day in and day out, 'twas the same. And the lads saw Yallery Brown flitting about o'

nights; and they saw the things working without hands o' days; and they saw that Tom's work was done for him, and theirs undone for them; and naturally they begun to look shy on him; and they wouldn't speak or come nigh him; and they carried tales to the master; and so things went from bad to worse.

For Tom could do nothing himself; the brooms wouldn't stay in his hand; the plough ran away from him; the hoe kept out of his grip. He thought that he'd do his own work after all, so that Yallery Brown would leave him and his neighbours alone. But he couldn't – true as death he couldn't. He could only sit by and look on, and have the cold shoulder turned on him, while the unnatural thing was meddling with the others, and working for him.

At last, things got so bad that the master gave Tom the sack, and if he hadn't, all the rest of the lads would have sacked him, for they swore they'd not stay on the same garth with Tom. Well, naturally, Tom felt bad – 'twas a very good place, and good pay too – and he was fair mad with Yallery Brown, as'd got him into such a trouble. So Tom shook his fist in the air and called out as loud as he could, 'Yallery Brown, come from the mools; thou scamp, I want thee!'

You'll scarce believe it, but he'd hardly brought out the words but he felt something tweaking his leg behind, while he jumped with the smart of it; and soon as he looked down, there was the tiddy thing, with his shining hair, and wrinkled face, and wicked, glinting black eyne.

Tom was in a fine rage, and he would have liked to have kicked him, but 'twas no good, there wasn't enough of it to get his boot against; but he said, 'Look here, master, I'll thank thee to leave me alone after this, dost hear? I want none of thy help, and I'll have nought more to do with thee – see now.'

The horrid thing broke into a screeching laugh, and pointed its brown finger at Tom. 'Ho, ho, Tom!' says he. 'Thou'st thanked me, my lad, and I told thee not, I told thee not!'

'I don't want thy help, I tell thee,' Tom yelled at him – 'I only want never to see thee again, and to have nought more to do with 'ee – thou can go.'

The thing only laughed and screeched and mocked, as long as

Tom went on swearing, but so soon as his breath gave out –

'Tom, my lad,' he said with a grin, 'I'll tell 'ee summat, Tom. True's true I'll never help thee again, and call as thou wilt, thou'lt never see me after today; but I never said that I'd leave thee alone, Tom, and I never will, my lad! I was nice and safe under the stone, Tom, and could do no harm; but thou let me out thyself, and thou can't put me back again! I would have been thy friend and worked for thee if thou had been wise; but since thou bee'st no more than a born fool, I'll give 'ee no more than a born fool's luck; and when all goes vicey-varsy, and everything agee – thou'lt mind that it's Yallery Brown's doing though m'appen thou doesn't see him. Mark my words, will 'ee?'

And he began to sing, dancing round Tom, like a bairn with his yellow hair, but looking older than ever with his grinning, wrinkled bit of a face:

> 'Work as thou will
> Thou'lt never do well;
> Work as thou may'st
> Thou'lt never gain grist;
> For harm and mischance and Yallery Brown
> Thou'st let out thyself from under the stone.'

Tom could never rightly mind what he said next. 'Twas all cussing and calling down misfortune on him; but he was so mazed in fright that he could only stand there shaking all over, and staring down at the horrid thing; and if he'd gone on long, Tom would have tumbled down in a fit. But by-and-by, his yaller, shining hair rose up in the air, and wrapt itself round him till he looked for all the world like a great, dandelion puff; and it floated away on the wind over the wall and out o' sight, with a parting skirl of wicked voice and sneering laugh.

And did it come true, say'st thou? My word! but it did, sure as death! He worked here and he worked there, and turned his hand to this and to that, but it always went agee, and 'twas all Yallery Brown's doing. And the children died, and the crops rotted – the beasts never fatted, and nothing ever did well with him; and till he was dead and buried, and m'appen even afterwards, there was no end to Yallery Brown's spite at him: day in and day out he used to hear him saying —

> 'Work as thou wilt
> Thou'lt never do well;
> Work as thou may'st
> Thou'llt never gain grist;
> For harm and mischance and Yallery Brown
> Thou'st let out thyself from under the stone.'

From *More English Fairy Tales* collected and edited by Joseph Jacobs

On a Cat Who Has Chewed His Master's Lute Strings

Pusse I will curse thee; may'st thou dwell
With some dry Hermit in a cell
Where rat neere peeped, where mouse neere fedd
And flies go supperless to bed;
Or with some close par'd Brother, where
Thou'lt fast each Sabboath in the yeare;
Or else, prophane, be hanged on Munday,
For butchering a mouse on Sunday;
Or may'st thou tumble from some tower,
And miss to light upon all fower,
Taking a fall that may untie
Eight of nine lives, and let them flye.

Thomas Master 1603–43

pity the poor spiders
by archy

(Archy is a cockroach who types his poems by hopping up and down on the keys, but he can't manage capital letters or punctuation)

i remember some weeks ago
meeting a middle aged spider
she was weeping
what is the trouble i asked
her it is these cursed
fly swatters she replied
they kill off all the flies
and my family and i are starving
to death it struck me as
so pathetic that i made
a little song about it
as follows to wit

twas an elderly mother spider
grown gaunt and fierce and grey
with her little ones crouched beside her
who wept as she sang this lay
curses on these here swatters
that kills off all the flies
for me and my little daughters
unless we eats we dies

swattin and swatting and swattin
tis little else you hear
and soon well be dead and forgotten
with the cost of living so dear

my husband he up and left me
lured off by a centipede
and he says as he bereft me
tis wrong but ill get a feed

and me a working and working
scouring the streets for food
faithful and never shirking
doing the best i could

curses on these here swatters
what kills off all the flies
me and my poor little daughters
unless we eats we dies

only a withered spider
feeble and worn and old
and this is what
you do when you swat
you swatters cruel and cold

i admit that some
of the insects do not lead
noble lives but is every
mans hand to be against them
yours for less justice
and more charity

archy

From *archy and mehitabel* by don marquis

Folklore And Magic

Folklore And Magic

Folk tales, or what are usually now called fairy tales, were not invented to amuse children, as so many people seem to think. They were stories that grown-up people really believed, told to one another and handed down to their children, who in turn passed them on again; and if every story-teller added a bit of embroidery of his own, who shall blame him?

A great many folk tales are about magic happenings, involving ordinary people and their dealings with witches and wizards and fairy people. There are still odd relics of these old beliefs in some superstitions of today. When you hear someone say: 'Of course, I never wear green, it's so unlucky,' they will probably have no idea that the idea arose because green was thought to be the colour of the fairies and to wear it put you in their power.

The fairy people, of which there were many kinds, were a separate race who had their home in the hills. They were not the sort with sequinned skirts and silver wands, which were a much later invention, but earthy, rather treacherous little things, like Yallery Brown. It was as well to beware of them, for there often turned out to be a catch in their favours.

Plant Lore

The primrose is the subject of a curious belief, particularly in East Suffolk and Sussex. There it is thought dangerous to bring fewer than thirteen primroses into the house when picking the first posy of spring. If a smaller number of flowers is picked, this will be the number of eggs which each hen belonging to the household will hatch that year. Malicious neighbours have been known to give a child a single primrose to take home: this would result in a single chick only being hatched. In some places only geese were thought to be affected. Primroses were a useful protection against witches and in the Isle of Man bunches were laid in the cowsheds on May

Day when witches were thought to be active. In Hampshire and the New Forest, woodmen treated their cuts with an ointment made of primrose flowers boiled with lard, and children eat the flowers to see fairies.

From *The Folklore of Plants* by Margaret Baker

Trefoil, Johnswort, Vervain and Dill,
Hinder witches of their will.

To Make Sure That No Dog Will Bite you place a leaf of the herb Hound's Tongue in your shoe beneath your big toe.

Warnings
Do not burn the wood of the elder. If you do the Devil will come down the chimney.

Never eat blackberries after the end of September. On the 1st of October the Devil spits on them.

If you swallow fern seed you will become invisible.

Francis Kilvert's Diary

Friday October 14 1870

. . . I turned in to old Hannah's, and sat with her an Hour talking over old times.
   She remembers how, when she was a child of six or eight, she would sit on a little stool by her grandfather's chair in the chimney corner listening while they (the old people) told their old world stories and tales of Faries (the fairies) in whom they fully believed . . .
   There was the Wild Duck Pool above Newbuilding . . . To this pool the people would come on Easter morning to see the sun dance and play in the water, and the angels who were at the

Resurrection playing backwards and forwards before the sun. There was also the 'sheep cot pool' below Wernwg, where Hob with his lantern was to be seen, only Hannah never saw him. But when People were going to market on Thursday mornings they would exhort one another to come back in good time lest they should be led astray by the Goblin Lantern, and boys would wear their hats the wrong way round lest they should be enticed into the fairy rings and made to dance. Then the story of the girl of Llan Pica who was led astray by the fairies and at last killed by them, and the story of the old man who slept in the mill trough at the Rhos Goch Mill, and used to hear the fairies come in at night and dance to sweet fiddles on the mill floor.

From the Diary of the Rev Francis Kilvert

The Ill-Wishing

There once lived a farmer in the Border country who seemed to have been born under a lucky star. His crops never failed, his cows seldom went dry, his butter was the sweetest for miles around, and his cream was so rich and thick you could skate a mouse on it. Even the great horse-chestnut tree that sheltered his snug farm house had more white candles and conkers to the twig than any round about. But his crowning joy was his pretty daughter.

Now there was a miller living near by, a squat, old, squinting fellow, that the girl couldn't abide.

'What, marry you?' she said when he asked her for the hundredth time. 'I'd as soon marry you as the tattybogle (scarecrow) in my father's field!'

Well, from that moment things began to go wrong for the farmer. The chestnut tree blew down in a mighty gale which tore the slates from his roof and flattened his corn and barley; the cows dropped their calves; and their milk was as thin and grey as the soapy water in his wife's wash-tub. But worst of all his pretty daughter fell ill with a little snickitty cough, that took the roses from her cheeks and the sparkle from her eyes.

'There's no help for it, my dear,' said the farmer to his wife. 'I shall have to consult the Wise Woman.' That was the polite name given to witches for it was as well to keep on the right side of such people or you never knew how they might get their own back at you. His wife nodded.

'Well, be sure to mind your manners and keep your fingers crossed!' she said, for every one knows that the sign of the cross will ward off evil magic.

The farmer knocked on the door of the Wise Woman's crazy, old cottage, for politeness sake. It hung on only one hinge and swung open as he did so, and there was the old woman sitting on a bench and sorting an apron full of nettles and nightshade, and a tangle of plants the farmer had never seen before, and at her feet a great, rangey, one-eyed, black cat patting a dandelion puff about the floor as though it was a mouse. The farmer crossed the fingers

of both hands inside his pockets to be on the safe side.

'What do you want with me?' sez the old woman.

The farmer told her about his good luck, which seemed to have changed over night to the worst luck in the world, and the cat stopped playing with the dandelion puff and squinnied up at him with his one green eye.

When the farmer had done the Wise Woman looked up, and her two eyes looked as green as the cat's in the dim light. She nodded slowly, and then she said:

'Is there anyone who wishes you ill?'

The farmer thought and thought, and then he remembered the miller.

The Wise Woman nodded again.

'This is what you must do,' she said. 'Kill the finest bullock of your herd, and cut out its heart. Carve on it the initials of the man who ill-wishes you, stick it full of pins and put it up the chimney. While you do it say these words . . .'

But what they were it is better not to write down in case they singe the paper. But when she had done she looked sideways at the cat who had been staring at the farmer with his one green eye all this time, and the cat gave a single yowl and turned to pat the dandelion puff again.

'And my pretty daughter?' asked the farmer.

'Do not let her sleep under your roof again,' said the Wise Woman. 'Send her where the winds blow from the North and the South and the West, and she will lose her snickitty cough.'

The farmer went home and did exactly what the Wise Woman had told him, and in a short time the miller came to his door looking so haggard and ill that the farmer felt quite sorry for him.

'Why, whatever ails you, man?' he asked.

'Right well you know!' said the miller. 'I can stand it no longer. Such pains I have in my heart, as though it was stuck as full of pins as a hedge-hog. Burning hot it is all the time. If only you'll ill-wish me no more, I'll do the same to you!'

So the farmer raked the ox's heart from the chimney and took out all the pins, which he put back in his wife's sewing box (pins were expensive in those days), and from that day his good luck came back again.

And his pretty daughter? Every evening she went riding over the hill on her white horse to a little house where the winds blow from the North and the West and the South, and where the treacherous East wind hardly ever finds its way, and in no time at all she lost her snickitty, little cough. I know because I have a house built in the very same place, which is why I was told this story by a very old lady who heard it from her grandmother, which is how all the best folk tales have found their way down to us.

Barbara Sleigh

The Witches' Song

First   'I last night lay all alone
Witch.   O' the ground, to hear a mandrake groan;
             And plucked him up, though he grew full low:
             And, as I had done, the cock did crow.'

Second   'And I ha' been plucking plants among
Witch.   Hemlock, henbane, adder's-tongue,
             Nightshade, moonwort, libberd's bane;
             And twice by the dogs was like to be ta'en.'

Third   'Yes, I have brought to help your vows,
Witch.   Horned poppies, cypress boughs.
             A fig-tree wild that grows on tombs,
             And juice that from the larch tree comes,
             The basilisk's blood, and the viper's skin;
             And now our orgies let's begin.'

From *A Masque of Queens* by Ben Jonson

Familiars

In the days when all the world believed in witchcraft, nearly every witch was thought to have one or more 'familiar': some animal, or even insect, which she used to find whether her magical ventures would succeed or not, or as a messenger to and from her master the Devil. Domestic familiars could be any living thing small enough to be kept indoors, which is why in so many stories a cat is described as a witch's companion.

Christina Hole tells us:

They usually took the shape of a cat, a rabbit, or something small enough to keep in the house without remark. Ales Cowley, an eighteenth-century witch, kept a toad in a cup under her bed, and Nanny Morgan, who was murdered in 1857, had a whole boxful of these creatures in her cottage. When John Steward, once schoolmaster of Knaresborough, was tried (for witchcraft which was against the law) in 1510 for invoking demons to find hidden treasure, a witness stated that he had three bumble bees, or what appeared to be such, which he kept under a stone in the earth and fed with drops of blood from his finger. Even a spider or fly might serve the purpose.

From *Witchcraft in England* by Christina Hole

The Old Conjurer

In Wales, a man-witch was called a conjurer. This story is told by an old Welsh woman at the end of the last century, written down exactly as she told it.

A man could be a witch, too, only he was called a Conjurer mostly.

Long, long ago, there was an old man living in a pretty little cottage near to the sea at Port Madoc. Old man he was, with white hair, and the cottage was 'nice iawn' (just right) and outside it was done with pink whitewash and blue slates, and the garden paths had borders of lovely sea shells to keep the flowers back from the paths, for the flowers were growing beautiful all over the place. Inside it was all as comfortable as a cabin, and all the furniture was solid mahogany.

The old man had been a sailor, and he had his compass and his sextant and a lots of ship's things by him still. He seemed to have plenty of money, and thought nothing of spending golden guineas at the market at Port Madoc, and people were wondering where he got his gold from, and were saying, 'Duwch, but this man he must have been a pirate, and he is still living on his murders!'

But at sunset, or when it was getting a bit dark-like, sailors would be seen going deceitful and quiet to that cottage, one at a time, very lonely and mysterious, and pretending not to be going there at all. They would be there for 'bout p'raps half-an-hour, and then would be coming away quick and happy.

And what was that old man doing with them sailors? Why! he was selling them fair winds! A good little breeze going the way they wanted it to.

Friends he was with the Prince of the Powers of the Air and making mock of Yr Arglwydd (The Lord God), and snapping his fingers! He had sold his soul to the Diawl (Devil) to be able to do such things, for he did do them, and the sailors were paying handsome.

And then one day a young sailor that he didn't like, who he was having a grudge against, came, and he pretended to sell him a fair wind, but instead he managed to make it a bad one, and the ship was wrecked, and the young sailor was drownded in the sea.

Well, one evening soon after, there was an awful sunset over Port Madoc. The sky was black and red, red as blood it was, and there were clouds flying across the sea looking like long black manes of hair, and the winds began to go howling and screaming, and the people of Port Madoc all went crowding to the Church, and began praying, 'Lord have mercy upon us,' but a most tremendous storm came on, and the sea came in all over the land roaring mountains high, and round the old man's cottage all the winds of the 'orld seemed thundering and shrieking at once, and some people said they heard a loud voice calling – 'I have come for my own to take my own,' and then night came, and the storms dropped, and there was silence.

Next morning the people were going and looking for the old man's cottage, but there was no cottage there, nothing! Nothing! Nothing at all, only a little sandhill with grass growing, and where the garden and lovely flowers had been, sand again, with just a few dead old star fish tossed about.

From *S'Nellie's Welsh Fairy Tales* by Eleanor Boniface

The Wheelbarrow Boy

Supposing magic happened today? Richard Parker, in his story 'The Wheelbarrow Boy', shows how it could at least enliven a dull school lesson.

'Now see here, Thomis,' I said. 'I've just about had enough of you. If you haven't settled yourself down and started some work in two minutes' time, I shall turn you into a wheelbarrow. I'm not warning you again.'

Of course, Thomis was not the only one: the whole class had the fidgets: he just happened to be the one I picked on. It was a windy day, and wind always upsets kids and makes them harder to handle. Also, I happened to know that Thomis's father had won a bit of money on the pools, so it was easy to understand the boy's being off balance. But it's fatal to start making allowances for bad behaviour.

After about three minutes I called out, 'Well, Thomis? How many sums have you done?'

'I'm just writing the date,' said the boy sullenly.

'Right,' I said. 'You can't say I didn't warn you.' And I changed him into a wheelbarrow there and then − a bright red, metal wheelbarrow with a pneumatic tyre.

The class went suddenly quiet, the way they do when you take a strong line, and during the next half-hour, we got a lot of work done. When the bell for morning break went, I drove them all out so as to have the room to myself.

'All right, Thomis,' I said. 'You can change back now.'

Nothing happened.

I thought at first he was sulking, but after a while I began to think that something had gone seriously wrong. I went round to the headmaster's office.

'Look,' I said, 'I just changed Thomis into a wheelbarrow and I can't get him back.'

'Oh,' said the Head and stared at the scattering of paper on his desk. 'Are you in a violent hurry about it?'

'No,' I said. 'It's a bit worrying, though.'

'Which is Thomis?'

'Scruffy little fellow – pasty-faced – always got a sniff and a mouthful of gum.'

'Red hair?'

'No, that's Sanderson. Black, and like a bird's nest.'

'Oh yes. I've got him. Well, now,' he looked at the clock. 'Suppose you bring this Thomis chap along here in about half an hour?'

'All right,' I said.

I was a bit thoughtful as I went upstairs to the Staff Room. Tongelow was brewing the tea, and as I looked at him I remembered that he had some sort of official position in the Union.

'How would it be if I paid my Union sub?' I said.

He put the teapot down gently. 'What've you done?' he asked. 'Pushed a kid out of a second-floor window?'

I pretended to be hurt. 'I just thought it was about time I paid,' I said. 'It doesn't do to get too much in arrears.'

In the end he took the money and gave me a receipt, and when I had tucked that away in my wallet I felt a lot better.

Back in my own room Thomis was still leaning up in his chair, red and awkward, a constant reproach to me. I could not start any serious work, so after about ten minutes I set the class something to keep them busy and then lifted Thomis down and wheeled him round to the Head.

'Oh, good,' he said. 'So the gardening requisition has started to come in at last.'

'No,' I said, dumping the barrow down in the middle of his carpet. 'This is Thomis. I told you . . .'

'Sorry,' he said. 'I'd clean forgotten. Leave him there and I'll get to work on him straight away. I'll send him back to you when he's presentable.'

I went back to my class and did a double period of composition, but no Thomis turned up. I thought the Old Man must have forgotten again, so when the bell went at twelve I took a peep into his room to jog his memory. He was on his knees on the carpet, jacket and tie off, with sweat pouring off his face. He got up weakly when he saw me.

'I've tried everything,' he said, 'and I can't budge him. Did you do anything unorthodox?'

'No,' I said. 'It was only a routine punishment.'

'I think you'd better ring the Union,' he said. 'Ask for legal aid – Maxstein's the lawyer – and see where you stand.'

'Do you mean we're stuck with this?' I said.

'You are,' said the Head. 'I should ring now, before they go to lunch.'

I got through to the Union in about ten minutes and luckily Maxstein was still there. He listened to my story, grunting now and then.

'You are a member, I suppose?'

'Oh yes,' I said.

'Paid up?'

'Certainly.'

'Good,' he said. 'Now let me see. I think I'd better ring you back in an hour or so. I've not had a case quite like this before, so I'll need to think about it.'

'Can't you give me a rough idea of how I stand?' I said.

'We're right behind you, of course,' said Maxstein. 'Free legal aid and all the rest of it . . . but, but I don't fancy your chances,' he said and rang off.

The afternoon dragged on, but there was no 'phone call from Maxstein. The Head got fed up with Thomis and had him wheeled out into the passage. At break-time I 'phoned the Union again.

'Sorry I didn't ring you,' said Maxstein when I got through to him again. 'I've been very busy.'

'What am I to do?' I asked.

'The whole thing,' said Maxstein, 'turns on the attitude of the parents. If they decide to prosecute I'll have to come down and work out some line of defence with you.'

'Meanwhile,' I said, 'Thomis is still a wheelbarrow.'

'Quite. Now here's what I suggest. Take him home tonight – yourself. See his people and try to get some idea of their attitude. You never know; they might be grateful.'

'Grateful?' I said.

'Well, there was that case in Glasgow – kid turned into a mincing machine – and the mother was as pleased as could be and refused to have him changed back. So go round and see, and let me know in the morning.'

'All right,' I said.

At four o'clock I waited behind and then, when the place was empty, wheeled Thomis out into the street.

I attracted quite a lot of attention on the way, from which I guessed the story must have preceded me. A lot of people I did not know nodded or said, 'Good evening,' and three or four ran out of shops to stare.

At last I reached the place and Mr Thomis opened the door. The house seemed to be full of people and noise, so I gathered it was a party in celebration of the pools.

He stared at me in a glazed sort of way for a moment and then made a violent effort to concentrate.

'It's Teddy's teacher,' he bawled to those inside. 'You're just in time. Come in and have a spot of something.'

'Well, actually,' I said, 'I've come about Teddy . . .'

'It can wait,' said Mr Thomis. 'Come on in.'

'No, but it's serious,' I said. 'You see, I turned Teddy into a wheelbarrow this morning, and now . . .'

'Come and have a drink first,' he said urgently.

So I went in, and drank to the healths of Mr and Mrs Thomis. 'How much did you win?' I asked politely.

'Eleven thousand quid,' said Mr Thomis. 'What a lark, eh?'

'And now,' I said firmly, 'about Teddy.'

'Oh, this wheelbarrow caper,' said Mr Thomis. 'We'll soon see about that.'

He dragged me outside into the yard and went up to the wheelbarrow. 'Is this him?' he said.

I nodded.

'Now look here, Teddy,' said Mr Thomis fiercely. 'Just you come to your senses this minute, or I'll bash the daylights out of you.' And as he spoke he began to unbuckle a heavy belt that was playing second fiddle to his braces.

The wheelbarrow changed back into Teddy Thomis and nipped

smartly down the garden and through a hole in the fence.

'There you are,' said Mr Thomis. 'Trouble with you teachers is you're too soft with the kids. Here, come in and have another drink.'

From Alfred Hitchcock's *Monster Museum*

Fattest-Of-All and Little-Thin-One

Once upon a time, long ago, there lived on the Gold Coast of Africa a girl who was so fat that she was made of nothing but oil. Luckily for her, in that part of the world the fatter a young woman was the more she was admired, so that Fattest-of-All, as she was called, was thought to be very beautiful indeed, and many were the young men who wanted to marry her. But there was one drawback to her fatness. She could not go out into the sun or she would melt away, and many a brave young chief returned to his village alone when he discovered this. For what use is a wife who cannot work for her husband in the fields?

At last there came a young man who owned many fields and much cattle, and when he saw Fattest-of-All he made up his mind to marry her, come what may.

'Have I not other wives who can work in the fields?' he said.

So he married Fattest-of-All and took her home to his village. Now Fattest-of-All had a little sister whom no one had ever sought in marriage because she was very thin, but though she was thin she was very wise, and she went too to keep her sister company. And on the long walk to their new home it was Little-Thin-One who saw to it that Fattest-of-All always walked in the shade.

At first all went well: Fattest-of-All carried out the many duties of a wife which can be performed in the shade, and when that was done she sat outside where it was coolest and fanned herself with a large leaf. But presently the other wives began to grumble, and the

chief among them, who could scarcely hide her jealousy of Fattest-of-All, said:

'Why should I hoe the stony ground, while you sit in the shade all day and twiddle your thumbs?'

'Because if I work in the sun I shall melt away!' said Fattest-of-All.

'Nonsense!' snapped the jealous wife, and she nagged and grumbled so much that at last Fattest-of-All consented to work in the fields for one morning, before the day grew too hot.

'I will weave you a wide hat of leaves,' said Little-Thin-One, 'then you will be protected from the sun.'

So Little-Thin-One wove her sister a wide hat of leaves, and they all three set out for the field together.

'You can hoe in that far corner,' said the jealous wife to Little-Thin-One. 'It is not fitting that you should hear the important matters that married women discuss.'

Little-Thin-One went off quite happily because she saw her sister was wearing the leafy hat.

They worked away for some time and the sun grew hotter and hotter.

'I don't see why you should be the only one to wear a hat,' said the jealous wife to Fattest-of-All. 'You might lend it to me for just a few minutes.'

'Very well,' said Fattest-of-All. 'I will lend it to you for a little, but you must promise to return it when I ask you.'

The jealous wife took the hat and put it on, and it grew hotter and hotter. Presently Fattest-of-All said faintly, 'Give me back my hat, I am melting in the sun!'

The jealous wife saw that she had indeed dwindled to half her usual size, but she would not give her back her hat. The sun grew hotter and hotter.

'Help! Help!' called Fattest-of-All presently, more faintly than before. 'Give me back my hat, I am melting in the sun!'

The jealous wife saw that she had melted so that she was no bigger than a cooking pot. But she would not give her back her hat.

When the sun was high in the heavens and the whole field seemed to quiver in the heat, Fattest-of-All began to call again:

'Help! Help! I am . . .' But that was all she said, because she had melted quite away. All that was left was one little drop of oil in the middle of a stone.

When Little-Thin-One came back and saw the jealous wife wearing the wide, leafy hat, and the little drop of oil in the middle of the stone, she guessed immediately what had happened. She collected the drop of oil very carefully, and put it in a jar, and then she searched and searched where Fattest-of-All had been working, and lo and behold, in the shade of a leaf where the sun had not been shining on it, she found her sister's left big toe. This too, she put into the jar, and then she filled the jar with cool water and took it back to the village and told the husband what had happened.

'Is there nothing I can do to bring back my lovely Fattest-of-All, Little-Thin-One?' he asked in sorrow.

'Why yes,' said Little-Thin-One. 'First you must send away the jealous wife, for it is an evil thing that she has done, and then you must fill the mouth of the jar with clay and put it in a cool, cool place for three months, and three days.'

So the jealous wife was sent back in disgrace to her parents, without the twenty head of cattle she had brought with her, and they were not at all pleased to see her. And at the end of the three months and three days Fattest-of-All stepped from the jar, if anything twice as fat as before, and in her husband's eyes twice as beautiful. And for my part, I only hope that Little-Thin-One found a husband just as loving.

From *North of Nowhere* by Barbara Sleigh

Science Fiction

Science Fiction

Science fiction stories come close on the heels of tales of magic. They are the modern form of fairy tale. After all, the flying carpet of the early story-teller was the forerunner of the space ship.

The first story, *Meteor* by John Wyndham, makes the point that if we were invaded by creatures from outer space we might not recognise who, or what, they were.

How would you try to survive on a planet inhabited only by animals who could neither see nor hear, but could make contact by thought-reading? In the second story, *The Odour Of Thought* by Robert Spreckly, Cleevy finds an ingenious but dangerous solution.

Meteor

The house shook, the windows rattled, a framed photograph fell off the mantelshelf and fell into the hearth. The sound of a crash somewhere outside arrived to drown the noise of breaking glass. Graham Toffts put his drink down carefully, and wiped the spilt sherry from his fingers.

'Did you hear that?' he asked unnecessarily. 'A small meteor, I fancy. I thought I saw a dim flash in the field beyond the orchard.' He withdrew.

Sally made after him. Graham, following more leisurely, found her firmly gripping her father's arm.

'No!' she was saying decisively. 'I'm not going to have my dinner kept waiting and spoiled. Whatever it is will keep.'

Mr Fontain looked at her, and then at Graham.

'Bossy; much too bossy. Always was. Can't think what you want to marry her for,' he said.

After dinner they went out to search with electric lamps. There was not much trouble in locating the scene of the impact. A small crater, some eight feet across, had appeared almost in the middle of the field. They regarded it without learning much, while Sally's terrier, Mitty, sniffed over the newly turned earth. Whatever had caused it had presumably buried itself in the middle.

'A small meteorite, without a doubt,' said Mr Fontain. 'We'll set a gang on digging it out tomorrow.'

*   *   *   *

Extract from Onn's Journal

As an introduction to the notes which I intend to keep, I can scarcely do better than give the gist of the address given to us on the day preceding our departure from Forta* by His Excellency Cottafts. In contrast to our public farewell, this meeting was deliberately made as informal as a gathering of several thousands can be.

'There is not one of you men and women who is not a volunteer,' he said, looking round his huge audience. 'Since you are individuals, the emotions which led you to volunteer may differ quite widely, but there is a common denominator for all — and that is the determination that our race shall survive.

'Tomorrow the Globes will go out.

'Tomorrow, God willing, the skill and science of Forta will break through the threats of Nature. In the past we have surmounted problem after problem to make this possible, but now we find ourselves faced with the gravest problem yet. Forta, our world, is becoming senile, but we are not. We are like spirits that are still young, trapped in a failing body . . .

'For centuries we have kept going, adapted, substituted, patched, but now the trap is closing faster, and there is little left to prop it open with. So it is now, while we are still healthy and strong, that we must escape and find ourselves a new home.

'The Globes will set out for the four corners of the heavens, and where they land they may find anything — or nothing. All our arts and skills will set you on your courses. But once you have left, we can do no more than pray that you, our seed, will find fruitful soil.'

He paused lengthily. Then he went on:

'In the hands of each and every one of you lies a civilisation.

* Onn gives no clue to Forta's position, nor as to whether it is a planet, a moon, or an asteroid.

Give it to others where it will help. Go forth, then. Go in wisdom, kindliness, peace and truth.

'And our prayers will go out with you into the mysteries of space . . .'

I have looked again through the telescope at our new home. Our group is, I think, lucky. It is a planet that is neither too young, nor too old. It shines like a blue pearl. Much of the part I saw was covered with water – more than two thirds of it, they tell me, is under water. It will be good to be in a place where irrigation and water supply are not one of the main problems of life. Nevertheless, one hopes that we shall be fortunate enough to make our landing on dry ground or there may be very great difficulties. . .

I shall go into the Globe, and the anaesthetic gas will lull me to sleep without me being aware of it. When I wake again it will be on our shimmering new world . . . If I do not wake, something will have gone wrong, but I shall never know that . . .

Very simple really – if one has faith . . .

This evening I went down to look at the Globes. What a staggering, amazing – one had almost said impossible – work they are! The building of them has entailed work beyond measure. They look more likely to crush the ground, sink into Forta herself than to fly off into space. The most massive things ever built! I find it almost impossible to believe that we can have built thirty of these metal mountains, and yet there they stand, ready for tomorrow . . .

It may well be that these are the last words I shall ever write. If not, it will be in a new world and under a strange sky that I continue . . .

*   *   *   *

'You shouldn't have touched it,' said the police inspector, shaking his head. 'It ought to have been left where it was until the proper authorities had inspected it.'

'And who,' inquired Mr Fontain coldly, 'are the proper authorities for the inspection of meteorites?'

'That's beside the point. You couldn't be sure it was a meteor, and these days a lot of things beside meteors can fall out of the sky.

Even now you've got it up you can't be sure.'

'It doesn't look like anything else.'

'All the same, it should have been left to us. It might be some device still on the Secret List.'

'The police, of course, knowing all about things on the Secret List?'

Sally considered it time to break in.

'Well, we shall know what to do next time we have a meteor, shan't we? Suppose we all go and have a look at it? It's in the outhouse now, looking quite unsecret.'

She led the way round to the yard, still talking, to stave off a row between the inspector and her father.

'It only went a surprisingly short way down, so the men were soon able to get it out. And it turned out to be not nearly so hot as we'd expected, either, so they could handle it quite easily.'

'You'd not say "quite easily" if you'd heard the language they used about the weight of it,' observed her father.

'It's in here,' said Sally, leading the party of four into a musty, single-storey shed.

The meteor was not an impressive sight. It lay in the middle of the bare, board floor; just a rugged, pitted, metallic-looking sphere something over two feet in diameter.

'The only kind of weapon it suggests to me is a cannon ball,' said Mr Fontain.

'It's the principle,' retorted the inspector. 'We have standing orders that any mysterious falling object is to remain untouched until it is examined by a war office expert. We have already informed them, and it must not be moved again until their man has had a look at it.'

Graham, who had hitherto taken no part, stepped forward and put his hand on it.

'Almost cold now,' he reported. 'What's it made of?' he added curiously.

Mr. Fontain shrugged.

'I imagine it's just an ordinary chunk of meteoric iron. The only odd thing about it to me is that it didn't come down with more of a bump. If it were any kind of secret weapon, it would certainly be a dull one.'

'All the same, I shall have to give orders that it is not to be moved until the war office man has seen it,' said the inspector.

They started to go back into the yard, but on the threshold he paused.

'What's that sizzling sound?' he inquired.

'Sizzling?' repeated Sally.

'Kind of hissing noise. Listen!'

They stood still, the inspector with his head a little on one side. Undeniably there was a faint, but persistent sound on a note just within the range of audibility. It was difficult to place. By common impulse they turned back to regard the ball uneasily. Graham hesitated, and then stepped inside again. He leaned over the ball, his right ear turned down to it.

'Yes,' he said. 'It is hissing.'

Then his eyes closed, and he swayed. Sally ran forward and caught him as he sagged. The others helped her to drag him out. In the fresh air he revived almost immediately.

'That's funny. What happened?' he asked.

'You're sure the sound is coming from that thing?'

'Oh, yes. Not a doubt about it.'

'You didn't smell anything queer?'

Graham raised his eyebrows: 'Oh, gas you mean? No, I don't think so.'

'H'm,' said the inspector. He turned a mildly triumphant eye on

the older man. 'Is it unusual for meteors to sizzle?'

'Er – I don't really know. I shouldn't think so,' Mr Fontain admitted.

'I see. Well, in the circumstances I suggest that we all withdraw – preferably to a well-shielded spot on the other side of the house, just in case – while we wait for the expert,' announced the inspector.

*　　*　　*　　*

Extract from Onn's Journal

I am bewildered. I have just woken. But has it happened – have we failed to start? I cannot tell. Was it an hour, a day, a year, or a century ago that we entered the Globe? No, it cannot have been an hour ago; I am sure of that by the tiredness of my limbs, and the way my body aches. We were warned about that:

'You will know nothing,' they said, 'nothing until it is all over. Then you will feel physically weary because your bodies will have been under great strains. That should pass quite soon, but we shall give you some capsules of concentrated food and stimulants to help you to overcome the effects more quickly.'

I have taken one capsule, and I begin to feel the benefit of it already, but it is still hard to believe it is all over. It seems such a short time ago that we climbed the long passage into the interior of the Globe and dispersed as we had been instructed. Each of us found his or her elastic compartment, and crawled into it. I released the valve to inflate the space between the inner and outer walls of my compartment. As the lining extended I felt myself lifted on a mattress of air. The top bulged down, the sides closed in, and so, insulated from the shock in all directions, I waited.

Waited for what? I still cannot say. One moment I lay there fresh and strong: the next I was tired and aching.

Only that, to indicate that one life has ended and a new one is about to begin. My compartment has deflated. The pumps have been exchanging gas for fresh air. That must mean that we are on that beautiful, shining, blue planet, with Forta only a speck in our new heavens.

I can hear the drills at work, cutting a way out for us. What, I wonder, shall we find? Who can tell what forms of life may exist here? One can scarcely expect to find real consciousness on a planet so young, but there may be the stirrings of intelligence here. They may be quite different from us, but we must remember that it is their world, and help them where we can. Our task must be to teach, to learn, to co-operate with them, and perhaps one day we may achieve a civilisation even greater than Forta's own . . .

*   *   *   *

'And just what?' inquired the inspector, 'do you think you are doing with that, Sergeant Brown?'

The police sergeant held the limp, furry body dangling by its tail.

'It's a cat, sir.'

'That's what I meant.'

'Well, I thought the war office gentleman might want to examine it.'

'And what makes you think the war office is interested in dead cats, Sergeant?'

The sergeant explained. He had decided to risk a trip into the outhouse to note developments, if any. Bearing in mind the inspector's suggestion of gas, he had tied a rope round his waist so that he could be dragged back if he were overcome, and crawled in, keeping as low as possible. The precautions had proved unnecessary, however. The hissing, or sizzling had ceased, and the gas had evidently dispersed. He had been able to approach the ball without feeling any effects whatever. Nevertheless, when he had come so close to it that his ear was almost against it he had noticed a faint buzzing.

'Buzzing?' repeated the inspector. 'You mean sizzling.'

'No, sir, buzzing. Like a circular saw, but as you might hear it from a very long way off.'

Deducing from this that the thing, whatever it was, was still active, the sergeant had ordered his constables away to cover, the other side of an earth bank. He had noticed the cat prowl into the yard just as they were settling down to a snack of sandwiches. It had gone nosing round the shed door, but he had not bothered about it. Half an hour later when he had finished his meal he had gone across to take another look. He discovered the cat lying close to the 'meteor'. When he brought it out, he had found it was dead.

'Gassed?' asked the inspector.

The sergeant shook his head. 'No, sir. That's what's funny about it.'

He laid the cat's body on top of the wall, and turned the head to expose the underside of the jaw. A small circle of black fur had been burnt away, and in the centre of the burn was a minute hole.

'H'm,' said the inspector. He touched the wound, and then sniffed at his forefingers. 'Fur's burnt, all right, but no smell of explosive fumes,' he said.

'That's not all, sir.'

The sergeant turned the head over to reveal an exactly similar blemish on the crown. He took a thin, straight wire from his pocket, and probed into the hole beneath the jaw. It emerged from the hole at the top of the head.

'Can you make anything of that, sir?' he asked.

The inspector frowned. A weapon of minute bore, at point blank range, might have made one of the wounds. But the two appeared to be entrance and exit holes of the same missile. A bullet did not come out leaving a neat hole like that, nor did it singe the hair about its exit.

'Have any theories?' he asked the sergeant.

'Beats me, sir,' the other told him.

'What's happening to the thing now? Is it still buzzing?' the inspector inquired.

'No, sir. There wasn't a sound from it when I went in and found the cat.'

'H'm,' said the inspector. 'Isn't it about time that war office man showed up?'

*　　*　　*　　*

Extract from Onn's Journal

This is a terrible place! As though we were condemned to some fantastic hell. Can this be our beautiful, blue planet that beckoned us so bravely? We cannot understand, we are utterly bewildered. We, the flower of civilisation, now cower before the hideous monstrosities that face us. How can we ever hope to bring order into such a world as this?

We are hiding now in a dark cavern while Iss, our leader, consults to decide our best course. Nine hundred and sixty-four of us depend on him. There were a thousand: this is the way it happened.

I heard the drill stop, then there was the clanking as it was dismantled and drawn from the long shaft it had bored. Soon after that came the call for assembly. We crawled out of our compartments, collected our personal belongings, and met in the central hall. Sunss, our leader then, himself called the roll. Everyone answered, except two poor fellows who had not stood the strain of the journey. Then Sunss made a brief speech.

He reminded us that what we had done was irrevocable. No one yet knew what awaited us outside the Globe. If it should happen that our party was divided, each group must elect its leader and act independently until contact with the rest was re-established.

'We do not know, and we shall never know, how the other Globes may have fared. So, not knowing, we must act as though we, only, had survived, and as if all that Forta has ever stood for is in our hands alone.'

It was he who led the way down the newly-bored passage, and he who first set foot on the new land. I followed with the rest, filled with such conflict of feelings as I have never known before.

And this world in which we have emerged: how can I describe it in all its alien qualities?

To begin with; it was gloomy and shadowed – and yet was not night time. Such light as there was came from a vast, grey panel hanging in the dusky sky: a square, bisected twice, by two dark bars into four smaller squares. In the murk over our heads it was possible to make out dimly-faint, darker lines.

The man beside me was nervous. He muttered something about a geometrical world lit by a square sun.

Soon we were all assembled outside the Globe, and waiting for Sunss to give directions. He was just about to speak when we were interrupted by a strange sound – a kind of regular soft padding, sometimes with a rasping scratch accompanying it. There was something ominous about it, and for a moment we were all frozen with apprehension – then, before we could move, the most fearsome monster emerged from behind our Globe.

The first we saw of it was an enormous face, thrusting round the side of the Globe, hanging in the air far above us. It was a sight to make the bravest shudder.

It was black, too, so that in the darkness it was difficult to be certain of its outline; but it widened across the top, and above the head itself one seemed to catch a glimpse of two towering, pointed ears. It looked down on us out of two vast, glowing eyes set somewhat aslant.

It paused for a moment, the great eyes blinked, and then it came closer. The legs which then came into view were like massive pillars, yet they moved with a dexterity and control that was amazing in anything that was so vast. Both legs and feet were covered with close-set fibres that looked like strands of shining, black metal. It bent its legs, lowering its head to look at us, and the fearful stench of its breath blew over us. The face was still more alarming at close quarters. It opened a cavern of a mouth; an enormous, pink tongue flicked out and back. Above the mouth, huge, pointed spines stood out sideways, trembling. The eyes that were fixed on us were cold, cruel, non-intelligent.

Until then we had been transfixed, now panic took some of us. Those nearest to it fell back hurriedly, and at that one of the monstrous feet moved like lightning. A huge black paw with sudden, out-thrust claws smacked down. When it drew back, twenty of our men and women were no more than smears on the ground.

We were paralysed, all of us except Sunss. He, forgetting his instructions about personal safety, ran towards the creature. The great paw rose, hovered, and struck again. Eleven more fell at that second murderous blow.

Then I noticed Sunss again. He was standing right between the paws. His fire-rod was in his hands, and he was looking up at the monstrous head above him. As I watched he lifted the weapon, and aimed. It seemed such folly against that huge thing, heroic folly. But Sunss was wiser than I. Suddenly the head jerked, a tremor

shook the limbs, and without a sound the monster dropped where it stood.

And Sunss was under it. A very brave man . . .

Then Iss took charge.

He decided that we must find a place of safety as soon as possible in case there were other such monsters lurking near. Once we had found that, we could start to remove our instruments and equipment from the Globe, and consider our next step.

After travelling a considerable distance we reached the foot of a towering and completely perpendicular cliff, with curious, regular rectangular formations on its face. At the base of it we found this cavern which seems to run a great distance both inwards and to both sides, and with a height which is oddly regular.

Here we have a refuge from monsters such as that which Sunss killed. It is too narrow for those huge paws to reach, and even the fearful claws could only rake a little way inside.

Later. A terrible thing has happened! Iss and a party of twenty went exploring to the cavern to see if they could find another way out other than on to the plain where our Globe lay.

Yes – lay! Past tense. That is our calamity.

After he had gone off, the rest of us waited, keeping watch. For some time nothing happened. Evidently, and mercifully the monster had been alone. It lay in a great, black mound where it had fallen, close to the Globe. Then a curious thing took place. More light suddenly poured over the plain. An enormous, hooked object descended upon the slain monster, and dragged it away out of sight. Then there was a thunderous noise which shook everything about us, and the light dimmed again.

Another, much longer period passed without any event. We were beginning to worry about what might have happened to Iss and his party, for they had been a long time away, when almost the worst thing that could happen to us occurred without warning.

Again the plain became lighter. The ground beneath us set up a reverberating rumble and shook so violently to a series of shocks that we were hard put to keep on our feet. Peering out from the cavern I saw a sight that even now I can scarcely credit. Forms, beside which our previous monster was insignificant: living, moving creatures reared up to three or four times the height of our vast Globe. I know this will not be believed – but it is the truth. Little wonder that the whole plain groaned and rumbled under the burden of such. They bent over our Globe, they put their fore-legs on it, and lifted it – yes, actually lifted that stupendous mass of metal from the ground. Then the shaking all about us became worse as they took its weight and tramped away on colossal feet.

Now our Globe with all its precious contents is lost. Our inheritance is gone. We have nothing now; nothing but our few trifling possessions, with which to start building our new world . . .

Nor was that the only calamity. Only a little later two of Iss's companions came back with a dreadful tale.

Iss had succeeded in reaching open country beyond the tunnels without the loss of a single man. It had been when they were on the way back to fetch us that catastrophe had overtaken them. They had been attacked by fierce, grey creatures about half the size of our first monster, which they guessed to be the builders of the tunnels. It was a terrible struggle, in which almost all the party perished before the monsters were overcome. Iss himself had fallen, and of all his men only these two had been left in a fit condition to make the journey back to us.

We have chosen Muin as our new leader. He has decided that we must go forward through the tunnels. The plain behind us is quite barren, our Globe is gone, if we stay here we shall starve; so we must try to get through to the open country beyond, trusting that Iss's sacrifice has not been in vain, and that there are no more grey monsters to attack us . . .

Is it so much that we ask — simply to live, to work, to build in peace . . .?

*   *   *   *

Graham looked in to see Sally and her father a couple of days later.

'I thought you might like an interim report on your "meteor",' he said to Mr Fontain.

'What was it, actually?' asked the older man.

'Oh, I don't say they've got that far. They established that it wasn't a meteor; but just what it really was still has them absolutely guessing.

'When they went over the thing carefully at the research place it appeared to be simply a solid ball of some metal on which there's been no report issued as yet. But in one place there was a hole, quite smooth, about half an inch in diameter, which went straight in, roughly to the middle. Well, they scratched their heads about the best way to tackle it, and decided in the end to cut it in half. So they rigged up an automatic sawing device in a pit and set it going, and we all retreated to a reasonable distance, just in case. Now they're all a bit more puzzled than they were before.'

'Why, what happened?' Sally asked.

'Well nothing actually happened. When the saw ran free we switched off and went back, and there was the ball lying in neat halves. But they weren't solid halves as they expected. There was a solid, metal rind about six inches thick, but then there was an inch or so of soft, fine dust, which has insulating qualities that seem to be interesting them quite a bit. Then inside a thinner metal wall was an odd formation of cells; more like a section of honeycomb than anything, only made of some flexible, rubbery material, and every one empty. Then a belt about two inches wide, divided into metal compartments this time, and crammed with all sorts of things – packs of minute tubes, things that look like tiny seeds, different sorts of powders that have spilled about when the thing came apart, and to which nobody's got round to examining properly yet, and finally a four inch space in the middle separated into layers by dozens of paper-thin fins, and absolutely empty otherwise.

'That's disappointing. It seemed so like a meteor – until it started sizzling,' said Mr Fontain.

'One of them has suggested that in a way it may be. A sort of artificial meteor,' Graham said. 'Though they feel that if something could be sent across space at all, surely it would be more intelligible.'

'It would be exciting if it were,' Sally said. 'I mean . . .'

She stopped suddenly at the sound of frenzied yapping outside. She jumped up as it changed to a long-drawn howl.

'That's Mitty!' she said. 'What on earth . . . ?'

The two men followed her out of the house.

'Mitty! Mitty!' she called, but there was no sign of the dog, nor sound from it now.

They made round to the left where the sound seemed to come from. Sally was the first to see the white patch lying on the grass beside the outhouse wall. She ran towards it calling; but the patch did not move.

'Oh, poor Mitty!' she said. 'I believe she's dead!'

She went down on her knees beside the dog's limp body.

'She is!' she said. 'I wonder what –' she broke off abruptly, and stood up. 'Something stung me! Oh, it hurts!'

She clutched at her leg, tears of anguish suddenly coming into her eyes.

'What on earth – ?' began her father, looking down at the dog. 'What are all those things – ants?'

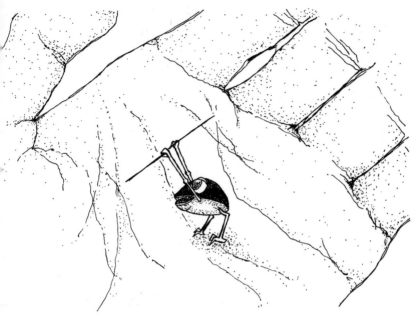

Graham bent down to look.

'No, they're not ants. I don't know what they are.'

He picked one of the little creatures up and put it on the palm of his hand to look at it more closely.

'Never seen anything like that before,' he said.

Mr Fontain beside him peered at it too.

It was a queer looking little thing, under a quarter of an inch long. Its body seemed to be an almost perfect hemisphere with the flat side below and the round top surface coloured pink, and as shiny as a ladybird's wing-cases. It was insect-like, except that it stood on only four short legs. There was no clearly defined head; just two eyes set in the edge of the shiny dome. As they watched, it reared up on two of its legs, showing a pale, flat underside, with a mouth set just below the eyes. In its forelegs it seemed to be holding a bit of grass or thin wire.

Graham felt a sudden searing pain in his hand.

'The little brute certainly can sting! I don't know what they are, but they're nasty things to have around. Got a spray handy?'

'There's one in the scullery,' Mr Fontain told him. He turned his attention to his daughter. 'Better?' he inquired.

'Hurts like blazes!' Sally said between her teeth.

'Just hang on a minute till we've dealt with this, then we'll have a look at it,' he told her.

Graham hurried back with the spray in his hand. He cast around and discovered several hundreds of the little pink objects crawling towards the wall of the outhouse. He pumped a cloud of insecticide over them and watched while they slowed, waved feeble legs, and then lay still. He sprayed the locality a little more, to make sure.

'That ought to fix them,' he said. 'Nasty, vicious little brutes. Never seen anything like them — I wonder what they were?'

Adapted from *Meteor* by John Wyndham

Tea in a Space-Ship

In this world a tablecloth need not be laid
On any table, but is spread out anywhere
Upon the always equidistant and
Invisible legs of gravity's wild air.

The tea, which never would grow cold,
Gathers itself into a wet and steaming ball,
And hurls its liquid molecules at anybody's head,
Or dances, eternal bilboquet,
In and out of the suspended cups up-
Ended in the weightless hands
Of chronically nervous jerks
Who yet would never spill a drop,
Their mouths agape for passing cakes.

Lumps of sparkling sugar
Sling themselves out of their crystal bowls
With a disordered fountain's

Ornamental stops and starts.
The milk describes a permanent parabola
Girdled with satellites of spinning tarts.
The future lives with graciousness.
The hostess finds her problems eased,
For there is honey still for tea
And butter keeps the ceiling greased.

She will provide, of course,
No cake-forks, spoons or knives.
They are so sharp, so dangerously gadabout,
It is regarded as a social misdemeanour
To put them out.

James Kirkup

The Odour of Thought

I'm putting down on the first oxygen planet I can find.'

He pulled down the Emergency Manual and looked up the Seergon Cluster. There were no colonies in the group, but the oxygen worlds had been charted. What was on them, aside from oxygen, no one knew. Cleevy expected to find out, if his ship stayed together long enough.

'I'll try 3-M-22,' he shouted over the mounting static.

'Take good care of the mail,' the postmaster howled back. 'I'm sending a ship right out.'

Cleevy made a good landing on 3-M-22; exceptionally good, taking into consideration the fact that his instruments were too hot to touch, his tubes were warped by heat, and the mail sack strapped to his back hampered his movements. Twenty feet above the planet's surface Mailship 243 gave up and dropped like a stone.

Cleevy held on to consciousness. The sides of the ship were turning a dull red when he stumbled through the escape hatch, the mail sack still firmly strapped to his back. He staggered one hundred yards, eyes closed. Then the ship exploded, and knocked him flat.

He stood up, took two more steps, and passed out completely.

When he recovered consciousness, he was lying on a little hillside, face-down in tall grass. He was in a beautiful state of shock. He looked round, and saw that a small animal was passing near him. It was about the size of a squirrel, but with dull green fur.

As it came close, he saw that it had no eyes or ears.

This didn't surprise him. On the contrary, it seemed quite fitting. Why in hell should a squirrel have eyes or ears?

Another animal approached, and this one was the size and shape of a wolf; but also coloured green. Parallel evolution? It didn't matter in the total scheme of things, he decided. This one, too, was eyeless and earless. But it had a magnificent set of teeth.

Cleevy watched with only faint interest. What does a pure intellect care for wolves and squirrels, eyeless or otherwise? The squirrel had frozen, not more than five feet from the wolf. The wolf approached slowly. Then, not three feet away, he seemed to lose the scent. He shook his head and turned a slow circle. When he moved forward again, he wasn't going in the right direction.

The blind hunt the blind, Cleevy told himself, and it seemed a deep and eternal truth. As he watched, the squirrel quivered; the wolf whirled, pounced, and ate it in three gulps.

What large teeth wolves have, Cleevy thought. Instantly the eyeless wolf whirled and faced him. Now he's going to eat me, Cleevy thought. It amused him to realise that he was the first human to be eaten on this planet.

The wolf was snarling in his face when Cleevy passed out again.

It was evening when he recovered. Long shadows had formed over the land, and the sun was low in the sky.

He got up on one knee, groggy, but in possession of his senses. What had happened? He remembered the crash as though it were a thousand years ago. The ship had burned, he had walked away and fainted. After that he had met a wolf and a squirrel.

He climbed unsteadily to his feet and looked around. He must have dreamed that last part. If there had been a wolf, he would have been killed. Glancing down at his feet, he saw the squirrel's green tail, and a little further away, its head.

He tried desperately to think. So there *had* been a wolf, and a

hungry one. If he expected to survive until the rescue ship came, he had to find out exactly what had happened, and why. Neither animal had eyes or ears. How did they track each other? Smell? If so, why did the wolf have so much trouble finding the squirrel?

He heard a low growl, and turned. There, not fifty feet away, was something that looked like a panther. A yellow-brown, eyeless, earless panther.

What a menagerie, Cleevy thought, and crouched down in the tall grass. This planet was rushing him along too fast. He needed time to think. How did these animals operate? Instead of sight, did they have a sense of location?

The panther began to move away.

Cleevy breathed a little easier. Perhaps, if he stayed out of sight, the panther . . . As soon as he thought the word *panther*, the beast turned in his direction.

What have I done, Cleevy asked himself, burrowing deeper into the grass. He can't see me or hear me. All I did was decide to stay out of his way . . .

Head high, the panther began to pace towards him. That did it. Without eyes or ears, there was only one way the beast could have detected him.

It had to be telepathic!

To test his theory, he thought the word *panther*, identifying it automatically with the animal that was approaching him. The panther roared furiously, and shortened the distance between them.

In a fraction of a second, Cleevy understood a lot of things. The wolf had been tracking the squirrel by telepathy. The squirrel had frozen – perhaps it had even stopped thinking! The wolf had been thrown off the scent – until the squirrel wasn't able to keep from thinking any longer.

In that case, why hadn't the wolf attacked him while he was unconscious? Perhaps he had stopped thinking. Probably there was more to it than that.

Right now, his problem was the *panther*.

The beast roared again. It was only thirty feet away, and closing the distance rapidly. All he had to do, Cleevy thought, was not to think of – was to think of something else. In that way, perhaps the – well, perhaps it would lose the scent. He started to think about all the girls he had ever known.

The panther stopped and pawed the ground doubtfully.

Cleevy went on thinking; about girls, and ships, and planets, and girls, and ships, and everything but panthers . . .

The panther advanced another five feet.

Damn it, he thought, how do you *not* think of something? You think furiously about stones and rocks and people and places and things, but your mind always returns to – but you ignore that, and concentrate on your sainted grandmother, your drunken old father, the bruises on your right leg (count them. Eight. Count them again. Still eight). And now you glance up, casually, seeing, but not really recognising the – anyhow, it's still advancing.

Cleevy found that trying *not* to think of something is like trying to stop an avalanche with your bare hands. It takes time, and practice. He had about fifteen feet left in which to learn how not to think of a . . .

Well, there are also card games to think about, and parties, and dogs, cats, mice, sheep, wolves (move away!) and bruises, battleships, caves, lairs, dens, cubs (watch out), p-*paramounts*, and tanta-

mounts and gadabouts and roundabouts and roustabouts and ins-and-outs (about eight feet) meals, food, fire, fox, fur, pigs, pokes, prams, and p-p-p-p- . . .

The panther was about five feet away now, and crouching for the spring. Cleevy couldn't hold back the thought any longer. Then, in a burst of inspiration, he thought: pantheress!

The panther, still crouching, faced him doubtfully.

Cleevy concentrated on the idea of a pantheress. *He* was a pantheress and what did this panther mean by frightening her that way? He thought about his (her) cubs, a warm cave, and pleasure of tracking down squirrels.

The panther advanced slowly and rubbed against Cleevy. Cleevy thought desperately, what fine weather we've been having, and what a fine panther this chap really is, so big, so strong, and with such enormous teeth.

The panther purred!

Cleevy lay down and curled an imaginary tail around him, and decided he was going to sleep. The panther stood by indecisively. He seemed to feel that something was wrong. He growled once, deep in his throat, then turned and loped away.

The sun had just set, and the entire land was a deep blue. Cleevy found that he was shaking uncontrollably, and on the verge of hysterical laughter. If the panther had stayed another moment . . .

He controlled himself with an effort. It was time for some serious thinking.

Probably every animal had its characteristic thought-smell. A squirrel emitted one kind, a wolf another, and a human still another. The all-important question was, could he be traced only when he thought of some animal? Or could his thought-pattern, like a smell, be detected even when he was not thinking of anything in particular?

He'd just have to wait and see. The panther probably wasn't stupid. It was just the first time that trick had been played on him.

Any trick will work – once. Cleevy lay back and stared at the sky. He was too tired to move, and his bruised body ached. What would happen now, at night? Did the beasts continue to hunt? Or was there a truce of some sort? He didn't care. To hell with squirrels, wolves, panthers, lions, tigers, and reindeer.

He slept.

The next morning, he was surprised to find himself still alive. So far, so good. Cheerfully, he walked to his ship.

All that was left of Mailship 243 was a pile of twisted metal strewn across the scorched earth. Cleevy found a bar of metal, felt the weight of it, and slid it into his belt below the mail sack. It wasn't much of a weapon, but it gave him a certain confidence.

The ship was a total loss. He left, and began to look for food. In the surrounding countryside there were several fruit-bearing shrubs. He sampled one warily, and found it tart but not unpleasant. He gorged himself on fruit, and washed it down with water from a nearby stream. He hadn't seen any animals, so far. Of course, for all he knew, they could be closing in on him now.

He avoided the thought and started looking for a place to hide until the rescue ship came. He tramped over the gentle rolling hills, looking for a cliff, a tree, a cave. But the amiable landscape presented nothing larger than a six-foot shrub.

By afternoon he was tired and irritated, and scanning the skies anxiously. Why wasn't the ship here? It should take no longer than a day or two, he estimated, for a fast, emergency ship to reach him.

If the postmaster was looking on the right planet.

There was a movement in the sky. He looked up, his heart racing furiously. There was something there! It was a bird. It sailed slowly over him, balancing easily on its gigantic wings. It dipped once, then flew on.

It looked amazingly like a vulture.

He continued walking. In another moment, he found himself face to face with four blind wolves. That took care of one question. He *could* be traced by his characteristic thought smell. Evidently the beasts of this planet had decided he wasn't too alien to eat.

The wolves moved cautiously towards him. Cleevy tried the trick he had used the other day. Lifting the metal bar out of his belt, he thought of himself as a female wolf searching for her cubs. Won't one of you gentlemen help me find them? They were here only a few minutes ago. One was green, one was spotted, and the other . . .

Perhaps these wolves didn't have spotted cubs. One of them leaped at Cleevy. Cleevy struck him in mid-air with his bar, and the wolf staggered back. Shoulder to shoulder, the four closed in.

Desperately Cleevy tried to think himself out of existence. No use. The wolves kept on coming.

Cleevy thought of a panther, *he* was a panther, a big one, and he was looking forward to a meal of wolf.

That stopped them. They switched their tails anxiously, but held their ground. Cleevy growled, pawed the earth and stalked forward. The wolves retreated, but one started to slip in behind him.

He moved sideways, trying to keep from being circled. It seemed that they really didn't believe him. Perhaps he didn't make a good panther. They had stopped retreating. One was behind him, and the others stood firm, their tongues lolling out on their wet, open jaws. Cleevy growled ferociously, and swung his club. A wolf darted back, but the one behind him sprang, landed on the mail sack, and knocked him over.

As they piled on, Cleevy had another inspiration. He imagined himself to be a snake, very fast, deadly, with poison fangs that could take a wolf's life in an instant. They were off him at once. Cleevy hissed, and arched his supple neck. The wolves howled angrily, but showed no inclination to attack.

Then Cleevy made a mistake. He knew that he should stand firm and brazen it out. But his body had its own ideas. Involuntarily he turned and sprinted away.

The wolves loped after him and, glancing up, Cleevy could see the vultures gathering for the remains. He controlled himself and tried to become a snake again, but the wolves kept coming.

The vultures overhead gave him an idea. As a spaceman he knew what the land looked like from the air. Cleevy decided to become a bird. He imagined himself soaring, balanced easily on an updraught, looking down on the green rolling land.

The wolves were confused. They ran in circles, and leaped into the air. Cleevy continued soaring, higher and higher, backing away slowly as he did so.

Finally he was out of sight of the wolves, and it was evening. He was exhausted. He had lived through another day. But evidently his gambits were only good once. What was he going to do tomorrow, if the rescue ship didn't come?

After it grew dark, he lay awake for a long time, watching the sky. But all he saw were stars. And all he heard was the occasional growl of a wolf, or the roar of a panther dreaming of his breakfast.

Morning came too soon. Cleevy awoke still tired and unrefreshed. He lay back and waited for something to happen. Where was the rescue ship? They had had plenty of time, he decided. Why weren't they here? If they waited too long, the panther . . .

He shouldn't have thought it. In answer, he heard a roar on his right. He stood up and moved away from the sound. He decided he'd be better off facing the wolves . . .

He shouldn't have thought that either, because now the roar of the panther was joined by the howl of a wolf pack.

Cleevy met them simultaneously. A green-yellow panther stepped daintily out of the underbush in front of him. On the other side, he could make out the shapes of several wolves. For a moment, he thought they might fight it out. If the wolves jumped the panther, he could get away.

But they were interested only in him. Why should they fight each other, he realised, when he was around, broadcasting his fears and helplessness for all to hear? The panther moved towards him. The wolves stayed back, evidently content to take the remains. Cleevy tried the bird routine, but the panther, after hesitating a moment, kept on coming.

Cleevy backed towards the wolves, wishing he had something to climb. What he needed was a cliff, or even a decent-sized tree . . .

But there were shrubs! With inventiveness born of desperation, Cleevy became a six-foot shrub. He didn't really know how a shrub would think, but he did his best.

He was blossoming now. And one of his roots felt a little wobbly. The result of that last storm. Still, he was a pretty good shrub, taking everything into consideration. Out of the corner of his branches, he saw the wolves stop moving. The panther circled him, sniffed, and cocked his head to one side.

Really now, he thought, who would want to take a bite out of a shrub? You may have thought I was something else, but actually, I'm just a shrub. You wouldn't want a mouthful of leaves, would you? And you might break a tooth on my branches. Who ever heard of panthers eating shrubs? And I *am* a shrub. Ask my mother. She was a shrub, too. We've all been shrubs, ever since the Carboniferous Age.

The panther showed no signs of attacking. But he showed no signs of leaving either. Cleevy wondered if he could keep it up. What should he think about next? The beauties of spring? A nest of robins in his hair?

A little bird landed on his shoulder.

Isn't that nice, Cleevy thought. He thinks I'm a shrub, too. He's going to build a nest in my branches. That's perfectly lovely. All the other shrubs will be jealous of me.

The bird tapped lightly at Cleevy's neck.

Easy, Cleevy thought. Wouldn't want to kill the tree that feeds you.

The bird tapped again, experimentally. Then, setting its feet firmly, proceeded to tap at Cleevy's neck with the speed of a pneumatic hammer.

A damned woodpecker, Cleevy thought, trying to stay shrublike. He noticed that the panther was suddenly restive. But after the bird had punctured his neck for the fifteenth time, Cleevy couldn't help himself. He picked up the bird and threw it at the panther.

The panther snapped, but not in time. Outraged, the bird flew around Cleevy's head, scolding. Then it streaked away for the quieter shrubs.

Instantly, Cleevy became a shrub again, but that game was over. The panther cuffed at him. Cleevy tried to run, stumbled over a wolf, and fell. With the panther growling in his ear, he knew that he was a corpse already.

The panther hesitated.

Cleevy now became a corpse to his melting finger-tips. He had been dead for days, weeks. His blood had long since drained away. His flesh stank. All that was left was rot and decay. No sane animal would touch him, no matter how hungry it was.

The panther seemed to agree. He backed away. The wolves howled hungrily, but they too were in retreat.

Cleevy advanced his putrefaction several days. He concentrated on how horribly indigestible he was, how genuinely unsavoury. And there was conviction in the back of his thought. He honestly didn't believe he would make a good meal for anyone.

The panther continued to move away, followed by the wolves. He was saved! He could go on being a corpse for the rest of his life, if necessary ... And then he smelled *truly* rotten flesh. Looking around, he saw that an enormous bird had landed beside him.

On Earth, it would have been called a vulture.

Cleevy could have cried at that moment. Wouldn't anything work? The vulture waddled towards him, and Cleevy jumped to his feet and kicked it away. If he had to be eaten, it wasn't going to be by a vulture.

The panther came back like a lightning bolt, and there seemed to be anger and frustration on that blank, furry face. Cleevy raised his

metal bar, wishing he had a tree to climb, a gun to shoot, or even an electric torch to wave . . .

A Torch!

He knew at once that he had found the answer. He blazed in the panther's face, and the panther backed away, squealing. Quickly Cleevy began to turn in all directions, devouring the dry grass, setting fire to the shrubs.

Now the panther and the wolves darted away.

Now it was his turn! He should have remembered that all animals have a deep instinctive dread of fire. He was going to be the greatest fire that ever hit this place!

A light breeze came up and fanned him across the rolling land. Squirrels fled from the underbush and streaked away from him. Families of birds took flight, and panthers, wolves and other animals ran side by side, all thought of food driven from their minds, wishing only to escape from the fire – to escape from him!

Dimly, Cleevy realised that he had now become truly telepathic himself. Eyes closed, he could see on all sides of him, and sense what was going on. As a roaring fire he advanced, sweeping everything before him. And he could *feel* the fear in their minds as they raced away.

It was fitting. Hadn't man always been the master, due to his adaptability, his superior intelligence? The same results obtained here too. Proudly he jumped a narrow stream three miles away, ignited a clump of bushes, flamed, spurted . . .

And then he felt the first drop of water. It was raining.

He burned on, but the drop became five, then fifteen, then five hundred. He was drenched, and his fuel, the grass and shrubs, were soon dripping with water.

He was being put out.

It just wasn't fair, Cleevy thought. By rights he should have won. He had met this planet on its own terms, and beaten it – only to have an act of nature ruin everything. Cautiously the animals were starting to return.

The water poured down. The last of Cleevy's flames went out. Cleevy sighed, and fainted.

'A fine job. You held on to your mail, and that's the mark of a good postman. Perhaps we can arrange a medal.'

Cleevy opened his eyes. The postmaster was standing over him, beaming proudly. He was lying on a bunk, and overhead he could see curving metal walls. He was on the rescue ship.

'What happened?' he croaked.

'We got you just in time,' the postmaster said. 'You'd better not move yet. We were almost too late.'

Cleevy felt the ship lift, and knew that they were leaving the surface of 3-M-22. He staggered to the port, and looked at the green land below him.

'It was close,' the postmaster said, standing beside Cleevy and looking down. 'We got the ship's sprinkler system going just in time. You were standing in the centre of the damnedest grass fire I've ever seen.' Looking down at the unscarred green land, the postmaster seemed to have a moment of doubt. He looked again, and his expression reminded Cleevy of the panther he had tricked.

'Say – how come you weren't burned?'

From *The People Trap* by Robert Sheckley

Acknowledgements

For permission to reprint the stories, poems and extracts in this book thanks are due to the following:

George Allen & Unwin Ltd and J. R. R. Tolkein for the poem 'The Mewlips' from *The Adventures of Tom Bombadil*.

George Allen & Unwin Ltd for 'Squids', an extract from *The Kon-Tiki Expedition* by Thor Heyerdahl.

The Bodley Head Ltd for the extract from *Beowulf, Dragon Slayer* by Rosemary Sutcliff.

George Bull and Penguin Classics (1956) for the translation of the extract from *The Autobiography of Benvenuto Cellini*.

Jonathan Cape Ltd and the Estates of Kenneth Walker and Geoffrey Boumphrey for 'The Scub', an extract from *The Log of the Ark*.

Jonathan Cape Ltd and F. R. Fletcher for two extracts from *The Diary of the Reverend Francis Kilvert*.

William Collins Sons & Co Ltd for 'Fattest-of-All and Little-Thin-One', from *North of Nowhere* by Barbara Sleigh.

Curtis Brown Ltd, London, on behalf of the author, Richard Parker, for 'Wheelbarrow' Boy.

J. M. Dent & Sons Ltd and the Trustees for the copyright of the late Dylan Thomas for 'The Carol Singers', an extract from *Quite Early One Morning*.

Faber & Faber Ltd for 'Pity the Poor Spiders', from *archy and mehitabel* by Don Marquis.

Andrew Haggard and Grower Books for 'The Haunting of Avenbury Church', an extract from *Dialect and Local Usages of Herefordshire*.

The Hamlyn Publishing Group Ltd for 'Butterfly Hunting in Dalmatia' from *Advice to Spies* by Sir Robert Baden-Powell, and also 'The Extra Hand' from *Sea Phantoms* by Warren Armstrong.

The Hutchinson Publishing Group Ltd for 'Old Madame', an extract from *Early Reminiscences* by S. Baring-Gould.

John Hynam for 'A Legion Marching By', from *The Eighth Ghost Book* published by Barrie & Jenkins Ltd.

Professor James Kirkup for permission to reprint his poem 'Tea in a Spaceship'.

Macmillan Ltd, London and Basingstoke, for 'Adventures with a Leopard', an extract from *The Life of Mary Kingsley* by Stephen Gwynn.

Macmillan Ltd, London and Basingstoke, and the Estate of Sir James Frazer for 'The Folklore of Dreams', an extract from *The Golden Bough*.

John Murray Ltd, Jonathan Cape Ltd and Baskervilles Investments Ltd for 'Pterodactyls', an extract from *The Lost World* by Sir Arthur Conan Doyle.

John Murray Ltd for 'Ghostlore of the Gilbert Islands' from *A Pattern of Islands* by Sir Arthur Grimble.

A. D. Peters & Co, London, on behalf of the author, Robert Sheckley, for 'The Odour of Thought' from *The People Trap*.

The Duke of Portland for an extract from the book, *Men, Women and Things*, published by Faber & Faber Ltd.

St Martin's Press Inc, New York, for 'Familiars', an extract from *Witchcraft in England* by Christina Hole.

Shire Publications Ltd for 'Primroses', an extract from *The Folklore of Plants* by Margaret Baker.

John Wyndham and Michael Joseph Ltd for 'Meteor', adapted from the story of that name from *The John Wyndham Omnibus*.

If, through inability to trace the present copyright holders, any copyright material is included for which permission has not been given, apologies are tendered in advance to those concerned.